Lecture Notes in Economics and Mathematical Systems

489

Springer
Berlin
Heidelberg
New York
Barcelona
Hong Kong
London
Milan
Paris
Singapore
Tokyo

Thomas Steger

Transitional Dynamics and Economic Growth in Developing Countries

 Springer

Author

Dr. Thomas Steger
DGZ Deka Bank
Economics Research Department
Mainzer Landstraße 16
60325 Frankfurt, Germany

H D
8 2
. S 8 2 4 5
2 0 0 0

This study was supported by the Friedrich-Naumann-Foundation with financial
of the German Federeal Ministry of Education and Research.

Library of Congress Cataloging-in-Publication Data

Steger, Thomas, 1966-
    Transitional dynamics and economic growth in developing countries / Thomas Steger.
        p. cm. -- (Lecture notes in economics and mathematical systems, ISSN 0075-8442 ; 489)
    Includes bibliographical references.
    ISBN 3540675639 (softcover : alk. paper)
        1. Economic development--Mathematical models. 2. Consumption
    (Economics)--Mathematical models. 3. Endogenous growth (Economics)--Mathematical
    models. 4. Equilibrium (Economics)--Mathematical models. 5. Developing
    countries--Economic conditions. 6. Developing countries--Economic policy. I. Title. II.
    Series.

    HD82 .S8245 2000
    338.9'009172'4--dc21

                                                                    00-032975

ISSN 0075-8442
ISBN 3-540-67563-9 Springer-Verlag Berlin Heidelberg New York

Springer-Verlag Berlin Heidelberg New York
a member of BertelsmannSpringer Science+Business Media GmbH

© Springer-Verlag Berlin Heidelberg 2000
Printed in Germany

"Gedruckt mit Unterstützung der Deutschen Forschungsgemeinschaft D467"
Typesetting: Camera ready by author
Printed on acid-free paper   SPIN: 10770908   41/3143/du   543210

Foreword

Since the renaissance of growth theory in the late 1980s, when Robert
Lucas and Paul Romer published their pioneering papers, an impressive
number of models have been developed. For years economic growth has
been one of the most active fields in economic research and economists'
understanding of growth has improved considerably during this time.
Since the emergence of 'New Growth Theory' economists faced the
challenge to model the transition towards long-run equilibria in closer
accordance with the stylised facts. In addition, a more sophisticated
analysis of convergence in the cross-section of countries has emerged. All
in all, theory can now reproduce a huge variety of growth patterns which
fit the data of international growth experiences.

Still, the difference between growth patterns of industrialised and developing countries goes beyond the capability of most of these new models. Growth theorists tend to focus on stationary structures rather than
long-lasting systematic changes (only the Schumpeterian view on economic growth in industrialised countries taken by Aghion and Howitt is
of the latter kind). However, it is not impossible to construct models
which capture elements of economic development in a satisfactory way
and combine this with a long-run perspective of developed countries.

In this study Thomas Steger develops examples of 'new growth models' which meet these requirements. He takes Gersovitz's view, according
to which "*[t]he development process is one of transition*", literally and
integrates it elegantly into particular growth models. The role of consumption in low-income countries is the key element which is common to
the different models. In standard growth models a decrease in consumption raises investment or innovation and therefore accelerates growth.
Steger explores the consequences of subsistence consumption and productive consumption in low-income countries. The influence of changes
in consumption is assumed to vanish in the long run. In other words, it
matters for the transition process but does not affect long-run balanced
growth.

This book enriches the literature on economic growth with models which treat transition towards long-run growth as an independent topic. The resulting implications of the transition process make these models an important contribution to the theory of economic growth and development.

Prof. Dr. Karl-Josef Koch
University of Siegen

Contents

1 Introduction

In the wake of endogenous growth theory, economic growth in developing countries (DCs) has been increasingly analysed by means of theoretical growth models. On this occasion, the growth process has been interpreted predominantly as representing balanced-growth dynamics (e.g. Azariadis and Drazen, 1990 and Becker, Murphy, and Tamura, 1990). These approaches are theoretically appealing because they demonstrate the possibility of multiple dynamic equilibria with strong implications for the prospects of economic development in low-income countries (Rebelo, 1992 and Benhabib and Gali, 1995). In addition, the models are empirically plausible to the extent that they are in line with the empirical finding of non-convergence in per capita incomes across the world (Romer, 1989, Section 2.1). At the same time, these approaches have some difficulties in explaining other empirical regularities of growth applying to the lower range of per capita income, e.g. a continuously increasing saving rate as income per capita rises and a positive correlation between the growth rate and the level of per capita income (ß-divergence). In contrast, according to a fundamentally different approach, the process of economic growth can be interpreted as representing mainly transitional dynamics towards a balanced-growth equilibrium. This strand of growth models can potentially explain specific aspects of growth in DCs without conflicting with the empirical regularities mentioned above.

The treatise in hand consists of one preliminary chapter and three main chapters. The common object of investigation of the main chapters is the process of aggregate economic growth in DCs. Moreover, the main chapters are based on the view that the process of growth, especially in the case of low-income countries, can be regarded as a transition towards a balanced-growth equilibrium, which might take a long period of time. It is further supposed that, even at the aggregate level, DCs possess special characteristics which are relevant to the analysis of growth. These comprise subsistence consumption, productive consumption, and 'endogenous control variables'. Accordingly, in Chapter 3 the implications of subsistence consumption are analysed against the background of the stylised facts of economic growth in DCs. The requirement of subsistence consumption necessitates a modification of the standard preference formulation. The resulting quantitative in addition to the qualitative convergence implications as well as the interactions with other essential mechanisms of growth and convergence are investigated comprehensively. In Chapter 4 the hypothesis of productive consumption, i.e. the notion that consumption activities enable the satisfaction of current needs and simultaneously increase the productive potential of labour, is incorporated into basic endogenous growth models. This hypothesis affects the production technology which is available to economic agents and modifies the intertemporal restrictions. On this occasion, the implications of the productive-consumption hypothesis for the intertemporal consumption trade-off and growth are investigated. Chapter 5 deals with the empirical analysis of the process of convergence to a balanced-growth equilibrium. The widespread view that those variables which are used to proxy the balanced-growth path, i.e. the control variables, can be considered as exogenous with respect to the growth process is refuted. Instead, these variables are considered as varying in the course of economic development. Consequently, their variation with income contains important information about the transition to the balanced-growth equilibrium rather than information about the balanced-growth equilibrium itself.

2 Preliminaries

Some of the basic issues which are important to the analysis of growth in DCs are discussed within this chapter. First, the empirical regularities of aggregate economic growth in DCs are summarised. For this purpose, a list of stylised facts is set up in Section 2.1, which mainly applies to the lower range of per capita income. Second, because the process of growth in DCs can be regarded as an object of investigation of development economics as well as growth theory, the relation between both fields of economics is clarified shortly in Section 2.2. Third, Section 2.3 presents an exposition of the main methodological foundations. The basic concepts, which are either implicitly or explicitly employed within the frame of dynamic macroeconomic theory, are presented in Section 2.3.1. Furthermore, modern growth theory can be regarded as a part of the neoclassical research programme, which is discussed in its essential features in Section 2.3.2. Finally, Section 2.3.3 concludes with the exposition of critical rationalism and stresses the demand for empirically refutable hypotheses as a result of theoretical analyses.

2.1 Stylised facts of aggregate growth in developing countries

Ever since Kaldor's (1961) study of economic growth it has been common to base the development of economic theory in general and growth theory in particular on a summary of the basic empirical regularities relevant to the problem of interest. The construction of theoretical models is designed to provide explanations of these '*stylised facts*'. This methodological procedure is best described by Kaldor's (1961, p. 178) own words: "..., *the theorist, in my view, should be free to start off with a 'stylized' view of the facts - i.e. concentrate on broad tendencies, ignoring individual detail, and proceed on the 'as if' method, i.e. construct a hypothesis that could account for these 'stylized' facts,...*" (quotation marks in original). Kaldor (1961, pp. 178/179) proposes six such stylised facts which characterise the phenomenon of economic growth. Romer (1989) shows that two of them are implied by others and therefore are redundant. Moreover, Romer (1989) enlarges Kaldor's original list of stylised facts by five other prominent features of the data.[1]

With regard to aggregate economic growth primarily applying to the lower range of per capita income there are distinct empirical regularities, which are only partly described by the list of stylised facts initially set up by Kaldor (1961) and enlarged by Romer (1989):[2]

(1) A considerable diversity in the growth rates of per capita income;
(2) a positive correlation between the saving rate and the level of per capita income; and
(3) a positive correlation between the growth rate and the level of per capita income, i.e. ß-divergence.[3]
(4) More generally, many authors report ß-divergence for the lower range of per capita income and ß-convergence for the upper range of per capita income, i.e. a hump-shaped pattern of growth.

In this section the list of stylised facts set up above is briefly illustrated and, if necessary, discussed in terms of empirical evidence.

Diversity in growth rates

The first empirical regularity corresponds to Kaldor's (1961) sixth stylised fact. In the case of low-income countries this empirical regularity is particularly marked as Lucas (1988, p. 4) states: *"Within the poor countries (low and middle income) there is enormous variability"* (brackets in original). Pritchett (1998, Section II) observes that the standard deviation of average annual growth rates from 1960-92 is twice as large for developing countries (DCs) compared to developed countries. This empirical regularity can be immediately visualised by means of the following scatterplot, which is familiar in growth literature.

---

[1] See Romer (1989, pp. 53-70) for a discussion.
[2] Especially for developing countries (DCs) there are empirical regularities applying to the structure of the economy which are not considered here. For this, see Kuznets (1973), Reynolds (1983), and Wichmann (1997, Chapter 3).
[3] This stylised fact seems to contradict Romer's seventh stylised fact according to which *"[i]n cross section, the mean growth rate shows no variation with the level of per capita income"*, Romer (1989, p. 55). However, Romer's stylised fact refers to the broad sample of 115 market economies. In addition, one should bear in mind that this assertion is mainly addressed to the neoclassical convergence implication which was one of the main empirical motivations for endogenous growth theory.

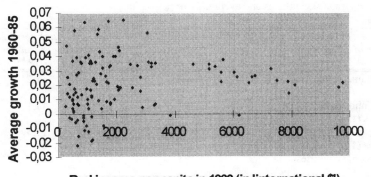

Real income per capita in 1960 (in 'international $')

Fig. 2.1. Average annual growth rates 1960-85[4]
Data source: Penn World Table Mark 5.6 (Summers and Heston, 1991).

Fig. 2.1 shows the average annual growth rate of per capita income over the time period 1960-85 on the vertical axis and the initial level of per capita income on the horizontal axis for a broad sample of countries (121 countries). The figure illustrates a considerable diversity in growth rates of per capita income including zero and even negative growth. In addition, the figure shows that this diversity is especially marked for low levels of per capita income.[5]

Positive correlation between the saving rate and per capita income

The empirical evidence in favour of a positive correlation between the saving rate and the level of per capita income is overwhelming. Thirlwall (1974, Chapter 7) reviews the older and Reichel (1993) the more recent literature.[6] As an illustration of the cross-country evidence, consider the following table.

Table 2.1 shows a clearly positive relation between the average saving rate and the average level of per capita income, with the largest increase in the saving rate occurring with the transition from low-income to lower middle-income countries. Obviously, the figures in Table 2.1 indicate a non-linear relation. The relation between the saving rate and the level of per capita income specifically appears concave.

---

[4] Usually, this kind of scatterplot uses the logarithm of per capita income on the horizontal axis (e.g. Barro and Sala-i-Martin, 1995, p. 27). For a similar scatterplot which uses per capita income instead of logarithmic per capita income on the horizontal axis see Baumol, Blackman, and Wolff (1989, p. 97).
[5] See Romer (1989, pp. 63-66) for further discussions.
[6] In addition, see Rebelo (1992, pp. 31-37) and Ogaki, Ostry, and Reinhart (1996, pp. 43-47).

Table 2.1. Average saving rates and average GNP per capita

Group of Countries [a] (number of countries)	Average GNP per person in 1985 $ [b]	Average personal saving as fraction of GDP [b]
Low-income-countries (16)	1,324	11.2
Lower middle-income countries (16)	2,806	17.1
Upper middle-income countries (11)	6,166	19.5
High-income countries (15)	12,293	21.1

Source: Ogaki, Ostry, and Reinhart (1996, pp. 44/45).
[a] Classification of economies according to World Bank (1994).
[b] For details see Ogaki, Ostry, and Reinhart (1996, pp. 44/45).

ß-Divergence

A positive (negative) correlation between the growth rate and the level of per capita income is described as ß-divergence (ß-convergence). Furthermore, a rise (fall) in the dispersion of per capita income over time, usually measured by the standard deviation of per capita income, is described as σ-divergence (σ-convergence) (e.g. Sala-i-Martin, 1996b, p. 1020). For the following discussion it is important to notice that ß-divergence is a necessary condition for the occurrence of σ-divergence.[7]

Cross-country estimates of ß-convergence or ß-divergence are usually based on the entire sample or sub-samples of the Penn World Tables (PWT, Summers and Heston, 1991) which include developing as well as industrialised economies. Empirical studies which exclusively analyse sub-samples of low-income countries are very rare.[8] According to Baumol (1986, pp. 1078/1079), industrial countries appear to belong to one convergence club, middle-income countries to a less pronounced, separate convergence club, and low-income countries actually diverged in the course of time. Zind (1991) runs cross-country regressions based on a sub-sample of the PWT for 89 less developed countries (LDCs) for the time interval 1960-80. He finds (unconditional) ß-divergence.[9] Cho (1994, Section II) divides the Summers-Heston data set into two half-sized sub-

---

[7] It is, however, not a sufficient condition for σ-divergence (Sala-i-Martin, 1996, p. 1021). For a more detailed discussion about the concepts of conditional and unconditional ß-convergence see Section 5.2.1.
[8] In contrast, a large number of empirical studies analyse conditional ß-convergence for sub-samples of high income countries; for details see Section 5.2.
[9] However, the convergence coefficient does not significantly differ from zero (Zind, 1991, p. 721). In addition see Baumol, Blackman, and Wolff (1989, pp. 302/303) who run a piecewise regression for the lower income group finding divergence as well.

samples with 48 LDCs and 47 developed countries. The partial correlation between the average growth rate and the initial level of per capita income is significantly positive for the lower sub-sample which indicates ß-divergence.[10] Moreover, Romer (1986, pp. 1008) demonstrates that there is a positive trend in growth rates for 11 now developed countries using the long-run data from Maddison (1979) which cover the time interval 1870-1978 (similarly, de la Fuente, 1997, pp. 26/27).

As has been noted above, the occurrence of σ-divergence for a specific time period necessarily requires the existence of ß-divergence within this time period. With regard to σ-divergence, the empirical evidence can be illustrated very easily. The subsequent figure displays the evolution of the standard deviation of the logarithmic per capita income over time for the group of 'poor' and 'middle-income' countries.[11]

Fig. 2.2 illustrates two points: First, the degree of inequality is higher for the group of 'poor' countries compared to the group of 'middle-income' countries.[12] Second, the disparity rose steadily over time, indicating continuous σ-divergence. Although long-run data on national accounts are generally not available for the group of DCs, Pritchett (1997) shows that there must have been significant σ-divergence in the world distribution of income over the last 150 years. He determines a lower threshold for the level of per capita GDP below which survival is impossible. To demonstrate that divergence must be an empirical characteristic of the last 150 years of economic growth, he combines this information with current estimates of relative incomes across nations and historical growth rates of the now-rich nations (in addition, Pritchett, 1998, Section II).

---

[10] This result is roughly compatible with the proceeding Fig. 2.1. For the lower range of income (below \$2000), the growth rate of per capita income appears to be positively related to the level of per capita income.

[11] The figure is taken from Ben-David (1994) who uses the Summers and Heston (1988) data set. The group of poor countries comprises 82 countries with per capita income smaller than \$2000 in 1960. The group of middle-income countries comprises 15 with per capita incomes ranging from 25 to 60 per cent of the US income in 1960 (Ben-David, 1994, p. 5).

[12] The higher standard deviation of the larger group (poor countries) compared to the smaller group (middle-income countries) is statistically meaningful because of at least two reasons: (i) The value of per capita income separating both groups is fixed at \$2000 because there is a 'sizeable gap' (Ben-David, 1994, p. 5) and (ii) Ben-David (1994, p. 6) obtains qualitatively identical results by grouping countries on the basis of 20 percent intervals.

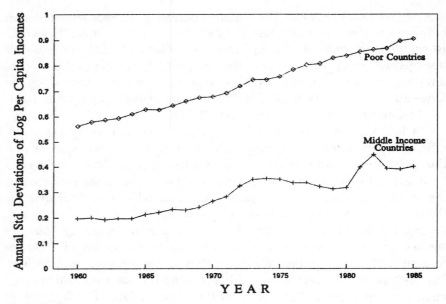

Fig. 2.2. Disparity
Source: Ben-David (1994, Figure 3).

Hump-shaped growth pattern

The empirical regularity of ß-divergence for the lower range of per capita income can be considered as being part of a more general pattern of growth. Indeed, a considerable amount of empirical evidence indicates that growth first accelerates as one moves from low- to middle-income countries and subsequently decelerates as one moves from middle- to high-income countries. Dollar (1992, Section 2) uses the Summers-Heston data for 114 economies (1960-85). The set of countries is divided into deciles based on 1960 level of income, with the richest countries in the first decile, and the poorest countries in the tenth decile (Dollar, 1992, p. 6). Subsequently, he estimates an univariate non-linear regression with the average growth rate of per capita income as the independent variable.[13] Fig. 2.3 shows the relation between growth rates and income levels for the deciles as well as the non-linear regression curve. The figure illustrates that there is a tendency of ß-divergence for the lower range and a tendency of ß-

---

[13] Dollar (1992, p. 6) states that "*...the regression line is a useful way to summarize the relationship between income level and growth rate...*" though "*..., the regression fit is not very good; the R^2 is only 0.10.*"

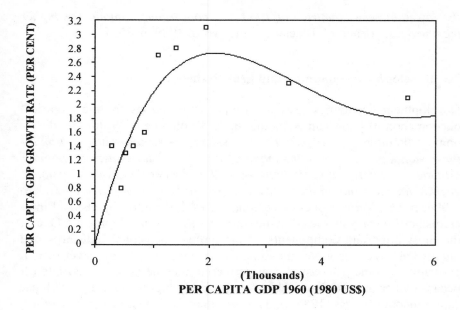

Fig. 2.3. Hump-shaped growth pattern
Source: Dollar (1992, Fig. 1).

convergence for the higher range of per capita income.[14] Moreover, Dollar (1992, p. 7) notes that "While the relationship depicted in Fig. 1 was estimated from cross-sectional data, it is interesting that it is broadly consistent with time-series data for countries that have successfully developed, like the United States and Japan. As these economies have industrialized, there has been a tendency for the growth rate to accelerate, then level off and slowly decline."

Furthermore, Easterly (1994, pp. 545-548) regresses the average annual growth rate of per capita income (1950-60) on, among other variables, the square of the initial level of logarithmic per capita income. The influence of this variable is significantly negative and therefore supports the hypothesis of a hump-shaped pattern of growth. Baumol, Blackman, and Wolff (1989) regress the ratio between the (logarithmic) real per capita income in 1980 and in 1950 on, among other variables, the square of real GDP per capita in 1950. The relevant coefficient is negative and significant. The authors conclude that "*[t]he results indicate divergence among*

---

[14] This result is compatible with the finding of convergence clubs among the richest countries (Baumol, 1986).

the lower income countries in 1950 and convergence among the higher income ones." (Baumol, Blackman, and Wolff, 1989, p. 303).[15]

2.2 Development economics and growth theory

Development economics seek to provide explanations for the empirical phenomenon of persistent economic underdevelopment. Within the development literature *'development'* is considered as representing *"...a multi-dimensional process involving major changes in social structures, popular attitudes, and national institutions, as well as the acceleration of economic growth, the reduction of inequality, and the eradication of poverty."* Todaro (1994, p. 16). Various one-dimensional as well as multi-dimensional indicators have been constructed to measure the level of development.[16] One of the most important components of the multi-dimensional indicators and one of the most important one-dimensional indicators is the level of real per capita income. Moreover, real per capita income is of special interest because other indicators of welfare are probably highly correlated with per capita income (Lucas, 1988, p. 3). Consequently, development economics and growth theory have common subjects of explanation which is the long-run evolution of per capita income.

The field of development economics is one of the most heterogeneous in economic theory and according to Todaro (1994, pp. 68/69) roughly comprises five approaches: (i) the stages-of-growth theory; (ii) the structural-change theory; (iii) the international dependence theory; (iv) the neoclassical theory (including neoclassical growth theory); and (v) the new or endogenous growth theory.[17] Growth theory in general considers persistent economic underdevelopment, narrowly defined in the sense of comparably low levels of per capita income, as a result of consistently inferior growth performances. Especially within the framework of endogenous growth theory, international differences in growth experiences are essentially explained on three different grounds. The first and second approach empha-

---

[15] The same authors find a hump-shaped relation between the growth rate of per capita income and the initial level of per capita income using a moving average approach (Baumol, Blackman, and Wolff, 1989, pp. 301/302). In addition, see Cho (1994, Section II) and Pritchett (1998) for similar results.

[16] As an example of a multi-dimensional indicator of development, consider the human-development-index (HDI) which is made up of three components: (i) life expectancy at birth; (ii) average adult literacy and mean years of schooling; and (iii) adjusted real per capita income (United Nations Development Program, 1992).

[17] For an overview see Todaro (1994, pp. 67-92). Endogenous growth theory will not be reviewed here since the number of excellent surveys is already substantial. See, for example, Romer (1989), Mankiw (1995), Jones and Manuelli (1997), and Barro (1997, Chapter 1).

sise balanced-growth dynamics whereas the third is based on transitional dynamics.

The first strand of models is marked by *unique dynamic equilibria*. The long-run growth rate of per capita income is determined endogenously by the economic structure and is dependent on the specific numerical values of the preference and technology parameters. According to this view, internationally divergent growth experiences are attributed to differences in preferences and technology. From a theoretical point of view, however, this way of reasoning is unsatisfying as Rebelo (1992, p. 7) pointed out. According to this methodological objection, modern growth theory, and modern macroeconomic theory in general, usually presumes or should presume 'some' symmetry between the economy under study and the rest of the world in order to rule out "...*explanations of differences in growth rates that are based solely on the existence of cross-country differences in preferences or technology.*" Rebelo (1992, p. 7). Without this restriction explanations of different growth experiences would become nearly tautological: Comparably superior growth performances would be considered as resulting from a more comfortable combination of those parameters which determine long-run growth and *vice versa*.[18]

The second strand of models emphasises *multiple dynamic equilibria*. These models demonstrate the possibilities of multiple (locally) stable dynamic equilibria. The lowest of these, i.e. the one which implies the lowest rate of growth, is called a *poverty trap* or a *low-level-equilibrium trap*. Accordingly, comparatively bad growth performances are interpreted as low-level-equilibrium traps (Azariadis, 1996, pp. 450/451).[19] As has been noted above, these approaches bear strong implications for the prospects of economic development in low-income countries (Rebelo, 1992 and Benhabib and Gali, 1995).

Both aforementioned approaches primarily focus on balanced-growth dynamics. Empirical growth dynamics are interpreted as dynamic equilibria rather than adjustment processes towards dynamic equilibria.[20] A basic

---

[18] Rebelo (1992, p. 7) further stresses that "*[t]his type of symmetry is conventional in modern macroeconomic theory but it is foreign to the development economics tradition. Most of the models used in development economics emphasize the unique features of underdeveloped countries.*" However, as long as different policies and institutional set-ups can be shown to have long-run growth effects, international differences in growth rates can meaningfully be explained by differences in these determinants. For explanations in this vein see Easterly, King, Levine, and Rebelo (1992) and Easterly (1994).

[19] Azariadis (1996) surveys growth models which imply low-level-equilibrium traps.

[20] These approaches have difficulty in explaining the 'turning point' at which a country first begins to exhibit a persistent upward trend in per capita income (Reynolds, 1983). Based on a historical analysis of growth, Reynolds (1983) stresses the distinction between extensive and intensive growth and determines the turning point for a number of countries. More analytically, Sarel (1994) distinguishes between an old and a modern period. The old period

third possibility to explain persistent underdevelopment, defined narrowly, within the framework of growth theory consists of interpreting real-world growth dynamics as representing *transition processes* to dynamic equilibria. Obviously this attempt at an explanation depends heavily on the rate of convergence implied by the growth models under study. Different growth experiences can only be represented sensibly as adjustment processes to a dynamic equilibrium if the implied rate of convergence is sufficiently low and the transition period is accordingly long. This view underlies the neo-classical growth theory. However, this theory suffers at least from two shortcomings: First, the implication of (conditional) ß-convergence seems to be inconsistent with the growth experiences of low-income countries and second, the neoclassical growth model implies comparably large values for the rate of convergence, i.e. short transition periods, when parameterised with empirically consistent values.[21]

2.3 Methodological foundations

2.3.1 Essential concepts in growth theory

2.3.1.1 Dynamic equilibrium

Irrespective of whether real-world processes of growth are interpreted as representing transitional or balanced-growth dynamics, the concept of 'dynamic equilibrium' is undoubtedly essential for growth theory. A *dynamic* or *long-run equilibrium* is defined as a situation in which the growth rates of all the endogenous variables are constant (e.g. Lucas, 1988, p. 9).[22] For conceptual clarity, two different forms are distinguished. A dynamic equilibrium which implies zero growth of per capita income is labelled a *steady state* while a dynamic equilibrium with positive per capita income growth is labelled a *balanced-growth equilibrium*. Additionally, there are dynamic models whose long-run behaviour is characterised by an *asymp-*

---

is characterised by zero per capita income growth while the modern period obeys positive growth of per capita income. This is accomplished within the frame of a neoclassical model by assuming a discrete jump in the growth rate of technical progress from zero to a positive constant (Sarel, 1994, pp. 7/8).

[21] For further details on the neoclassical convergence implication see Section 5.2.

[22] The growth rates can be identical though this is not necessary. Formally, let $\dot{x} = F(x)$

be an ordinary differential equation system defined on an open set $W \subset R^n_+$ which describes the evolution of a dynamic model. A dynamic equilibrium with constant growth rates $\widetilde{g} = (g_1, ..., g_n)$ accordingly is a curve C so that

$$C = \{x_i \in R^n \big| F_i(x) = g_i x_i \, \forall i\} \text{ (Koch, 1997, p. 10).}$$

totic balanced-growth equilibrium. At no point in time balanced growth is effectively realised. However, balanced growth occurs as an asymptotic property, i.e. the economy converges asymptotically towards a balanced-growth path.[23]

For the sake of completeness, a second equilibrium concept is to be explained which is related to the time dimension. According to Phelps (1987) 'equilibrium' in economics is basically an expectational concept. It implies that the expectations of individuals are fulfilled and hence optimal plans based on these correct expectations are maintained (Phelps, 1987, pp. 177/178). Therefore, it is useful to distinguish between intertemporal and dynamic equilibria. An *intertemporal equilibrium* is defined as a situation in which expectations about future variables (prices and quantities) are continuously fulfilled and hence individuals have no reason to alter their intertemporally optimal plans. The models employed in growth theory are predominantly deterministic and economic actors are assumed to have perfect foresight, which is equivalent to the assumption of rational expectations under complete information. In addition, most of these models rely on sound microeconomic foundations and are neoclassical in the sense that there are no price rigidities. Consequently, these models imply intertemporal equilibria at each point in time.[24]

In the course of a critical discussion of the concept 'dynamic equilibrium' at least two questions arise: (i) What is the theoretical justification of this concept? (ii) How appropriate is this concept in explaining real-world phenomena of 'long-run growth'?

With regard to the theoretical justification of the concept 'dynamic equilibrium', there appears to be an asymmetry between one-sector and multi-sector growth models. Within the frame of one-sector growth models, a dynamic equilibrium is frequently a compelling property of the solution to the underlying optimal control problem. It is well known that the dynamic equilibrium of the Ramsey-Cass-Koopmans model, for example, is the only long-run solution which satisfies all optimum conditions.[25] In this view, the dynamic equilibrium is the natural long-run result of in-

---

[23] Models which are characterised by asymptotic balanced growth can be economically meaningful and emphasise the importance of transitional dynamics to a greater extent than balanced-growth dynamics. Examples are Jones and Manuelli (1990), linear growth with Stone-Geary preferences (see Chapter 3), and growth models with productive consumption (see Chapter 4).

[24] It should be noted explicitly that 'dynamic equilibrium' and 'intertemporal equilibrium' are completely separate concepts which focus on different criteria to define 'equilibrium' against the background of the time dimension.

[25] Every other solution would violate at least one of the conditions which have to be satisfied according to the maximum principle. One would violate the requirement that the costate variable has to be a continuos function of time while the other would violate the transversality condition (e.g. Maußner and Klump, 1996, pp. 130/131).

tertemporal optimisation under perfect foresight and not an *ad-hoc* imposed *a priori* requirement. Within the frame of multi-sector growth models, the situation appears different. In this case, a dynamic equilibrium has to be imposed as a technical *a priori* requirement in order to analyse a specific solution. Accordingly, Lucas (1988, p. 9) states "*I have never been sure exactly what it is that is 'balanced' along such a path, but we need a term for solutions with this constant growth rate property and this is as good as any.*" (quotation marks in original). Similarly, Jones and Manuelli (1997, p. 88) notice that the realisation of a balanced-growth path is "*...a nontrivial assumption, since, in general, two-sector models can exhibit very complex dynamics...*". The theoretical justification is thus vague and seems to be only justified by the fact that "*...this is as good as any.*" as Lucas (1988, p. 9) comments.

With respect to the second question raised above, it is useful to realise that the concept of dynamic equilibrium illustrates the notion of a long-run state of the economy which is characterised by persistent regularity without structural change (Koch, 1997, p. 9). In addition, the dynamic equilibrium or long-run state of the economy is considered to be *a priori* determined by the structure of the economy, possibly together with the initial conditions. According to this view, the adjustment process to the dynamic equilibrium does not affect the dynamic equilibrium itself.[26] This aspect appears theoretically questionable. In the course of economic development, interpreted as transitional dynamics, events which alter the long-run equilibrium, like technical revolutions, radical changes in the political system, and the emergence of new institutions, might occur. Consequently, this approach only offers a qualified explanation for the process of growth, i.e. the dynamics of an economy are explained to the extent that major structural changes do not occur.[27]

2.3.1.2 *Representative agent models*

The microfoundations of modern macroeconomic theory are widely viewed as an improvement over the theoretically unjustified behavioural assumptions underlying early macroeconomic models. Modern macroeco-

---

[26] It should be noted that there are theoretical approaches providing a completely different view: According to the path-dependency approach 'early' events in the course of economic development crucially determine the path of development; 'history matters' (North, 1989). Path-dependent processes result from positive feedback effects which are based mainly on increasing returns to scale, sunk costs, and positive network externalities (Arthur, Ermoliev, and Kaniovski, 1987).

[27] A similar problem arises in the course of comparative-static analysis. Regardless of the empirical relevance of the concept of (static) equilibrium, the use of this concept allows to describe "*...the direction in which some variables will move next, without however being able to say what their final resting place, if they have one, will be.*" Hahn (1984, p. 49).

nomic theory is extensively based on representative agent models which are used to analyse an 'artificial economy' composed of a number of identical agents whose behaviour can be summarised by that of a representative individual. Aggregate economic phenomena are modelled as the result of the choices of a representative agent who maximises his or her utility subject to several constraints. Various interpretations are possible: First, the representative agent can be interpreted as a hypothetical social planner (normative analysis). Second, it can be interpreted as a consumer-producer household (Robinson-Crusoe economy). The economy under study can also be interpreted as consisting of a number of separate identical consumer-worker households on the one hand and a number of identical firms on the other hand (positive analysis).[28]

It is clear that all phenomena which are essentially based on interpersonal heterogeneity (e.g. distributional aspects) cannot be analysed within this framework. The representative agent model is used instead to analyse some central macroeconomic phenomena such as intertemporal consumption decisions, capital accumulation, and growth. Nevertheless, there are some fundamental criticisms which mainly read as follows (Kirman, 1992, p. 118 and Turnovsky, 1996, p. 274): (i) The aggregation of diverse individual choices is only permissible under a set of extremely restrictive assumptions (Kirman, 1992, p. 120).[29] (ii) Consistent aggregation of individual preferences might be impossible (Arrow's impossibility theorem). In this case the preferences of the representative agent cannot legitimately be used for welfare considerations (Maußner and Klump, 1996, p. 29). (iii) Empirical tests of the representative agent models suffer from the fact that they effectively test a joint hypothesis which consists of the specific behavioural hypothesis implied by the model under study together with the additional hypothesis that macroeconomic phenomena are adequately described by a representative agent model.[30]

Replies to these methodological criticisms are principally based on two different grounds. First, the representative agent model is not intended to give a realistic picture of the real world. It is rather to be viewed as a method which tries to structure and understand macroeconomic interdependencies (Maußner and Klump, 1996, p. 29). The scientific appropriateness of this procedure should exclusively be assessed according to its empirical success or failure in reproducing the empirical phenomena under

---

[28] Romer (1989, pp. 70-75) shows the equivalence between the decentralised competitive equilibrium and the corresponding social planning problem within a general growth model.

[29] For a concise and non-formal overview of aggregation problems see Fisher (1987).

[30] In order to avoid this difficulty Kirman (1992, pp. 129) suggests that models should incorporate heterogeneous agents.

study.[31] Second, it is simply argued that "..., *the representative agent model is the best available at the present time,...*" Turnovsky (1996, p. 274). The development and application of heterogeneous agent models is to be considered as a comprehensive task for future research. Finally, Jones and Manuelli (1997, p. 86) stress that 'much of the intuition' developed within the representative agent framework still holds if heterogeneity among consumers is admitted. To sum up, if the representative agent framework is applied, it is important to be at least aware of the methodological problems which are inherent in it.[32]

2.3.2 Neoclassical research programme

According to Lakatos (1978), a scientific research programme consists of two components: the 'hard core' and the 'protective belt'.[33] The hard core contains empirically irrefutable assumptions while the protective belt contains auxiliary assumptions and refutable hypotheses (Blaug, 1992, p. 34). Specifically, the hard core of the neoclassical scientific research programme comprises at least methodological individualism and the postulate of rationality. At this level the expressions 'neoclassical growth theory' and 'endogenous growth theory' do not necessarily imply that these theories belong to different scientific research programmes. *Methodological individualism* states that social phenomena are the result of individual actions and individuals are considered to be capable of acting on their own authority. According to the *postulate of rationality*, individuals try to maximise a properly specified utility function subject to the constraints of endowments and technology.[34]

The claim for methodological individualism requires the analysis of the individual decision-making process. Accordingly, macroeconomic phenomena are explained on the grounds of microeconomic theories. This requirement is usually met by employing representative agent models, which have been discussed in the previous section. The postulate of ration-

---

[31] This kind of reasoning is in the spirit of Popper's (1934) falsificationism and Friedman's (1953) instrumentalism; for further discussion on this matter see Section 2.3.3.

[32] Even advanced textbooks concerned with macroeconomic and growth theory fail to mention these problems; see, for example, Barro and Sala-i-Martin (1995), Blanchard and Fischer (1989), and Romer (1996). Notable exceptions are Maußner and Klump (1996) and Turnovsky (1996).

[33] Lakatos (1978) argues that rather than single theories so-called scientific research programmes, i.e. more or less interconnected theories should be the units for making scientific appraisals.

[34] Becker (1971) further stresses the assumption of stable preferences. Consequently, social phenomena are explained by a change in income and relative prices. It should be noted that Becker (1971) extends the range of application of the 'economic approach' to all kinds of human behaviour.

ality, the second basic assumption of the neoclassical research programme, has been frequently attacked.[35] The main argument against it reads that the rationality principle is merely a metaphysical proposition which can neither be verified nor falsified. There are at least three important arguments with respect to this criticism: (i) According to Popper (1967), the principle of rationality, interpreted as an empirical law, is admittedly false. But it represents a good approximation of the real world and should therefore be used as a starting point of every model of social science.[36] (ii) Every science finally rests on metaphysical propositions which cannot be verified.[37] (iii) According to Friedman's methodology of instrumentalism, the validity or realism of assumptions is simply regarded as irrelevant. Theories serve as instruments to derive predictions about the class of phenomena which they intend to explain. Therefore, economic agents are considered to be acting as if they maximise a well specified utility function subject to constraints. The decision units are not regarded as necessarily conscious of their efforts to optimise utility (Friedman, 1953, p. 22 and Becker, 1971, p. 7). According to this view, the scientific validity of a theory is judged solely by its predictive power. If a theory fails repeatedly to predict the empirical phenomena in question it should be rejected, while in the case of successful prediction it is provisionally confirmed (Friedman, 1953).[38] In short, the principle of rationality is not regarded as a necessarily realistic assumption but instead it is seen as a heuristic concept to derive explanations or predictions about the real world.[39]

2.3.3 Critical rationalism

Growth theory is primarily designed to enhance our understanding of the growth process. The judgement of the epistemological value of a theory requires corresponding criteria, which are developed in the field of philosophy of science. The dominant and most convincing basic point of view within the philosophy of science is that of *critical rationalism* (Popper,

---

[35] For a concise review of the criticism of rationality see Blaug (1992, pp. 232/233).

[36] If a model is refuted by empirical observations, Popper (1967, p. 355) proposes to refuse the model and not the principle of rationality, because *"[w]ir lernen mehr, wenn wir unser Situationsmodell dafür verantwortlich machen."* In addition, if the principle of rationality is rejected, Popper argues, explanations in social science would be threatened to become arbitrary.

[37] Newtonian physics, for example, is based on the notion of absolute time and space (Blaug, 1992, p. 34).

[38] The argumentation of Friedman (1953) is very close to Popper's (1934) falsificationism without referring to it.

[39] Admittedly, for explanations which claim to be causal, 'rationality' must at least be regarded as a good approximation (Blaug, 1992, p. 92).

1934).[40] According to this normative methodological theory all empirical theories can be divided into two mutually exclusive classes: 'science' and 'non-science'. The demarcation criterion between these two classes is the basic possibility of falsification. Accordingly, synthetic propositions about the real world are regarded as science if they can, at least in principle, be refuted by empirical observations (Blaug, 1992, pp. 13/14).[41] The starting point for the justification of the falsifiability-criteria is the logical asymmetry between verification and falsification. Hypotheses, construed as universal propositions about the real world, can never be verified in general on the grounds of empirical observations, irrespective of the number of observations. On the other hand, the falsification of an empirical hypothesis is possible on the grounds of a single empirical refutation.[42] Epistemologically, this fundamental asymmetry between verification and falsification leads to the claim for theories which imply empirically refutable hypotheses. Otherwise those theories are without empirical content and consequently are regarded as non-scientific.

According to this basic methodological point of view, the scientific progress should advance as follows: Theories which intend to explain specific aspects of the real world are required to imply refutable hypotheses; i.e. they must compellingly rule out specific observable events. The scientific community should seek to falsify these theories instead of trying to verify them. In the case of successful falsification by empirical observation, the theory should be regarded as invalid. If repeated attempts of falsification fail, the theory in question should be regarded as provisionally accepted (Blaug, 1992, p. 24). It should be noted that the greater the generality of a theory, i.e. the wider the scope of its implications the easier is its falsification, provided that it is in fact false, and the greater is its scientific

---

[40] See Blaug (1992) and Rook, Frey, and Irle (1993) for alternative approaches.

[41] The demand for falsifiability as the demarcation criterion results from a critique of logical positivism. According to logical positivism, science starts with empirical observation and general theories are obtained by induction. The scientific validity is judged according to the success of verification.

[42] The famous example of white and black swans is illustrative: One can assert 'all swans are white' and could try to verify this hypothesis by searching for swans. However, irrespective of the number of white swans observed, the verification of the hypothesis is impossible. In contrast, the observation of only one black swan would falsify the hypothesis 'all swans are white'. The reason for the impossibility of verification lies in the 'problem of induction' interpreted as a logical method of concluding from a finite number of elements to the infinite number of possible ones. Induction in this sense is invalid, which was already recognised by Hume and taken up by Popper (1934). This is not to say that statistical inferences which clearly represent an inductive conclusion are inadmissible. The reason is that statistical inferences do not claim to be logically compelling (Blaug, 1992, pp. 15-17).

value. Hence, simplicity is a positive attribute of a theory because simple theories possess a higher empirical content.[43]

Nevertheless, this position of 'naive' or 'dogmatic' falsificationism requires some qualifications. First, it should be permissible in principle to further develop theories which have been falsified to account for the observed contradictions or 'anomalies'.[44] However, the modifications must not represent 'immunising stratagems'. That is, only those modifications which at least maintain the degree of empirical testability or falsifiability are regarded to be permissible (Blaug, 1992, pp. 18/19).[45] Second, a theory which is regarded as falsified should only be abandoned if a superior alternative is available (Rook, Frey, and Irle, 1993, p. 29). Third, in the case of probabilistic theories the logical asymmetry between verification and falsification is not strictly valid. The attempt of falsification of probabilistic hypotheses must necessarily be based on a methodological value judgement. By the choice of the level of significance of empirical tests, the scientist is forced to weigh the risk of rejecting a hypothesis which is in fact true (Type I error) against the risk of accepting a hypothesis which is in fact false (Type II error).[46]

This modified falsificationism appears to be the most convincing methodological procedure for scientific progress not only in natural but also in social science. Despite the qualifications described above the demand for theories which bear refutable hypotheses is indispensable in order to discriminate between empirically meaningful and empirically meaningless theories.[47] In accordance with this view, the implications of the growth models which are discussed in the Chapters 3 and 4 can be distinguished into two groups. The first group comprises implications which represent possible implications of the models. These might be interesting to the extent that they demonstrate the potential of the model under study to reproduce one of the stylised facts of economic growth. However, as far as these

---

[43] 'Simplicity of theories' in this view is not meaningful because of aesthetic or pragmatic reasons. It is instead meaningful because of epistemological reasons as Popper (1973, p. 103) states: *"Einfachere Sätze sind (wenn wir 'erkennen' wollen) deshalb höher zu werten als weniger einfache, weil sie mehr sagen, weil ihr empirischer Gehalt größer ist, weil sie besser überprüfbar sind."* (quotation marks and brackets in original).

[44] A famous example for this strategy in economics is the extension of the price theory by Becker (1965).

[45] In this context, it is important to mention the Duhem-Quine thesis which states that no individual scientific hypothesis is conclusively falsifiable, because the entire explanans (the particular hypothesis in conjunction with auxiliary statements) is tested (Blaug, 1992, p. 18).

[46] This is the essence of the Neyman-Pearson theory of statistical inference (Blaug, 1992, pp. 21/22 and Rook, Frey, and Irle, 1993, p. 30).

[47] The demand for 'working out' a theory's refutable hypotheses is not frequently emphasised in economics. For a notable exception see the textbook of Silberberg (1990).

implications are no compelling results, they do not represent refutable hypotheses. The second group comprises compelling implications which represent refutable hypotheses in the sense described above.

3 Economic growth with subsistence consumption [*]

3.1 Introduction

"The development process is one of transition." Gersovitz (1988, p. 383)

If one takes Gersovitz (1988) literally and is interested in an explanation of the process of economic growth and development in terms of growth theory, one is led to ask what class of growth models is consistent with this view. In addition, it is reasonable to ask what class of growth models is able to reproduce the main stylised facts of (aggregate) economic growth primarily applying to the lower range of per capita income, which have been discussed in Section 2.1 and are restated here for the readers convenience:

(1) A considerable diversity in the growth rates of per capita income;[48]
(2) a positive correlation between the saving rate and per capita income; and
(3) a positive correlation between the growth rate and the level of per capita income, i.e. ß-divergence.
(4) More generally, many authors report ß-divergence for the lower range of per capita income and ß-convergence for the upper range of per capita income, i.e. a hump-shaped growth pattern.

The theory of economic growth reveals two elementary forces of growth. They consist in an increase in total factor productivity (TFP) as a result of innovation, imitation, adoption, and adaptation on the one hand and the accumulation of reproducible inputs (physical as well as human capital) on the other hand.[49] Especially in the long run, the accumulation of

---

[*] This chapter is based on Steger (2000a).

[48] This corresponds to Kaldor's (1961) sixth fact.

[49] 'Ideas and objects' in the words of Romer (1993) or according to Klenow and Rodríguez-Clare (1997, p. 611) 'A versus K'. The discussion of the East Asian Miracle largely centred around the question whether this 'miracle' was primarily input driven or primarily caused

physical and human capital needs to be financed by internal saving.[50] Within the development literature, it is stressed that saving in the case of developing countries (DCs) is determined by the willingness to save as well as the ability to save (e.g. Hemmer, 1988, pp. 150-159). The usual constant-intertemporal-elasticity-of-substitution (CIES) formulation of preferences assumes that the entire income is disposable for saving. That is, these models abstract from the requirement of a minimum consumption level in order to sustain life. However, the requirement of subsistence consumption undoubtedly restricts the possibilities to substitute consumption intertemporally and hence the ability to save at least for the lower range of per capita income. Several questions arise which are of fundamental importance: Does the requirement of subsistence consumption influence the process of growth beyond this threshold? If so, how long does it take for the influence of subsistence consumption on growth to vanish? How does the requirement of subsistence consumption interact with other essential mechanisms of growth? The chapter in hand seeks to answer these questions systematically within the context of simple endogenous growth models with Stone-Geary preferences. In addition, it will be shown that these models provide a potential explanation of the stylised facts listed above. It is assumed that the economy under study is symmetric to the rest of the world with respect to preferences and technology. The aim of this methodological assumption is to rule out explanations of differences in growth experiences that are based solely on the existence of cross-country differences in preferences and technology.

This chapter is organised as follows: In Section 3.2, the concept of subsistence and its empirical importance is discussed concisely and a short overview of growth models with subsistence consumption is given. In Section 3.3, a linear growth model with Stone-Geary preferences is analysed comprehensively. The quantitative convergence implications are investigated in addition to the qualitative convergence implication. In Section 3.4, the basic model is extended by diminishing marginal returns to capital as well as by the general meaning of policy-induced distortions. Section 3.5 summarises and concludes with some final considerations.

---

by increases in the TFP. Young (1995) supports the view that an increase in inputs was the dominant force behind the economic progress observed for this group of countries.

[50] As far as specific consumption activities (nutrition, health efforts, and education) are productive, the accumulation of human capital does not necessarily require the renunciation of consumption (see Chapter 4). This aspect is ignored within this chapter.

3.2 The subsistence level of consumption

Subsistence is a widely-used concept with varying meanings and definitions. Sharif (1986) comprehensively surveys the concept, its importance in the context of different theories, and its measurement (in addition, Reynolds, 1983, Section II.A). Subsistence as a mode of production can be distinguished from subsistence as a mode of consumption. The first is usually defined as (mostly agricultural) production for home-consumption, while the latter denotes a standard of living that allows for the satisfaction of the minimum (physical and probably mental) basic needs of life. Three methods of the determination of the subsistence level of consumption can be distinguished: (i) The direct observation of the provision of subsistence consumption levels by the society (subsistence as a social norm); (ii) the scientific estimation of the physiological and mental requirements for sustaining life (Stigler, 1945 and World Bank, 1990); and (iii) the determination of subsistence consumption according to declarations or economic behaviour of individuals.[51]

The interpretation of subsistence as a mode of consumption corresponds to the concept of the poverty line, which is used to identify that part of the population which is regarded as absolutely poor. The theory of (absolute) poverty measurement is extensively based on the concept of the poverty line.[52] In order to determine the poverty line, usually a list of goods and services necessary for subsistence is made. Subsequently, that income which is necessary to purchase this basket of goods and services is calculated (e.g. Atkinson, 1987, p. 930). Accordingly, all people who dispose of an income which falls short of the poverty line are regarded as absolutely poor. The World Bank (1990) uses a consumption-based poverty line in order to define absolute poverty. The poverty line comprises two elements: First, the expenditure necessary to realise a minimum standard of nutrition and other basic necessities and second a further amount reflecting the cost of participation in everyday life of society (World Bank, 1990, p. 26).[53] Beside this distinction, two poverty lines are employed in order to distinguish between the 'poor' and the 'extremely poor'. The lower poverty line

---

[51] Sharif (1986, p. 568) reports the results of an empirical study which estimates a value of 0.6 for the income elasticity of 'declared subsistence' with respect to per capita income. This is an empirical indication for the possible endogeneity of the subsistence level of consumption.

[52] Absolute poverty refers to material needs irrespective of distributional issues, while relative poverty refers to income inequality. The poverty line is the basis for most measures of income poverty like the head count index, the poverty gap, and the severity of poverty (e.g. Ravallion, 1992).

[53] In addition, the World Bank (1990) stresses that the second component probably varies from society to society as well as with the level of per capita income (World Bank, 1990, p. 27).

amounts to $275, while the upper poverty line amounts to $370 in 1985 PPP prices (World Bank, 1990, p. 27). In addition, Ben-David (1994, p. 11) reports calculations from Stigler (1945), who estimates the subsistence level of consumption defined as the least-cost requirement for sustaining an individual's dietary needs as approximately $300 a year (in 1980 $).

The relevance of the obvious requirement of subsistence consumption for economic growth is straightforward. The requirement of subsistence consumption restricts the ability to save. Consequently, within the framework of all growth models which explain growth as the result of the accumulation of the reproducible factors, the restriction of the ability to save crucially influences the process of growth. Intuitively, this influence is greater the nearer an economy is located at subsistence. How appropriate or relevant is this concept? There are clearly other heavy burdens that can inhibit growth in these countries: Poor and deteriorating infrastructure, a bad institutional set-up, and macroeconomic instability. However, if a large part of the population is concerned with nothing else but staying alive, these other issues are of minor importance for the poorest economies (Ben-David, 1994, pp. 10/11).

Table 3.1. Per capita income in excess of subsistence

Group of countries[a] (number of countries)	GNP per capita[b]	Proportional difference I[c]	Proportional difference II[d]
Low-income economies (36)	320	0.14	-0.16
China and India (2)	340	0.19	-0.32
Other low-income (34)	280	0.02	-0.09
Lower-middle-income economies (34)	1,380	0.80	0.73
Upper-middle-income economies (14)	3,240	0.92	0.89
High-income economies (25)	17,080	0.98	0.98

Source: World Bank (1990, pp. 178-180).
[a] Country groups: Low-income economies: GNP per capita $\leq \$545$, Lower-middle-income economies: $\$545 <$ GNP per capita $\leq \$2,200$, Upper-middle-income economies: $\$2,200 <$ GNP per capita $< \$6000$ (World Bank, 1990, p. x).
[b] in 1988 Dollars.
[c] Proportional difference between GNP per capita and the lower poverty line.
[d] Proportional difference between GNP per capita and the upper poverty line.

In order to obtain an impression of the empirical relevance of subsistence consumption, the preceding Table 3.1 displays the proportional difference between per capita income and the subsistence level of consumption. The latter is first identified with the lower (proportional difference I) and second with the upper poverty line (proportional difference II) as used by the World Bank (1990). The third column shows that per capita income exceeds the lower poverty line for the group of low-income economies only marginally; the proportional difference I amounts to 0.14. Moreover, per capita income even falls short of the upper poverty line as shown in the fourth column; the proportional difference II amounts to -0.16 for the same group of economies.

Subsistence consumption considerations seem to be of minor importance for the middle-income economies [lower-middle income economies: 0.80 (prop. diff. I) and 0.73 (prop. diff. II), upper-middle-income economies: 0.92 (prop. diff. I) and 0.89 (prop. diff. II)]. For the high-income economies the requirement of subsistence consumption is nearly irrelevant [0.98 (prop. diff. I and II)]. The meaning of the requirement of subsistence consumption for intertemporal consumption decisions can be easily formalised by means of an intertemporal Stone-Geary utility function. The subsistence level of consumption, $\bar{c} > 0$, is interpreted as that amount of consumption which is a necessary prerequisite for sustaining life. Solely consumption which exceeds the subsistence level creates well-being, i.e. the instantaneous utility function is defined on the range $c \geq \bar{c}$:[54]

$$U[\{c(t)\}] = \int_0^\infty \frac{[c(t) - \bar{c}]^{1-\theta} - 1}{1 - \theta} \cdot e^{-(\rho - n) \cdot t} \, dt \, . \tag{3.1}$$

The instantaneous utility function in (3.1) is twice continuously differentiable and strictly concave, $u'(c) > 0$ and $u''(c) < 0$.[55] The intertemporal utility function assumes that consumption is additively separable and that the value of the utility functional converges to a finite value which requires $\rho > n$. The usual CIES function can be regarded as a special case of (3.1) with $\bar{c} = 0$, i.e. the requirement of subsistence consumption is ignored. This might approximately be justified in the case of developed countries. However, for developing countries subsistence consumption considerations are of major importance and should be taken into account within theoretical analyses. The instantaneous Stone-Geary utility function implies a constant elasticity of the marginal utility with respect to consumption in ex-

---

[54] The so-called Stone-Geary utility function is a generalisation of the Cobb-Douglas utility function. It was developed by Klein and Rubin (1948-49) and Samuelson (1948-49) and econometrically applied by Stone (1954) and Geary (1950).

[55] In addition, the Stone-Geary utility function is non-homothetic and implies linear expenditure systems. It is consistent with linear Engel curves and an elasticity of consumption expenditures with respect to income which is smaller than unity (e.g. Silberberg, 1990, pp. 406/407 and Chung, 1994, Section I.2).

cess of subsistence which equals $\sigma(c - \bar{c}) \equiv -\dfrac{u''(c - \bar{c}) \cdot (c - \bar{c})}{u'(c - \bar{c})} = \theta$. How-

ever, with respect to consumption the elasticity of the marginal utility is

$\sigma(c) \equiv -\dfrac{u''(c)c}{u'(c)} = \dfrac{\theta c}{c - \bar{c}}$. Consequently, the IES for two immediate points

in time, which equals the inverse of the elasticity of the marginal utility, reads as follows:[56]

$$\sigma(c)^{-1} \equiv -\frac{u'(c)}{u''(c)c} = \frac{c - \bar{c}}{\theta c} . \tag{3.2}$$

Several properties of the IES are noteworthy: (i) The IES is zero for consumption equal to the subsistence level of consumption; (ii) the IES increases with the level of consumption $c(t)$, hence (3.1) does not belong to the class of CIES utility functions; and (iii) the IES asymptotically converges to θ^{-1} as consumption per capita grows without bound. These properties make good economic sense. If income equals the subsistence level of consumption, the individual is simply unable to substitute consumption intertemporally and the IES equals zero. For an increasing income level the individual must first achieve subsistence consumption letting intertemporal considerations guide its decisions only for that portion of the budget which exceeds subsistence.

In order to address specific theoretical as well as empirical questions, Stone-Geary preferences have occasionally been applied within growth and development literature. This paragraph presents a comprehensive but concise survey of the different approaches: Nelson (1956) uses the notion of subsistence consumption to establish two essential elements of his low-level-equilibrium-trap model. These consist in the hypothesis concerning capital formation and population growth. Christiano (1989) uses a neoclassical model with preferences explicitly accounting for the requirement of subsistence consumption in which a trend is introduced in subsistence consumption to interpret the growth of Japan in the post-war period. According to Rebelo (1992), a 'broad class of endogenous growth models' is inconsistent with cross-country diversity in growth rates in the face of international capital markets. As a solution to this theoretical problem, Rebelo suggests a linear growth model with Stone-Geary preferences. King and Rebelo (1993) study the transitional dynamics of the neoclassical growth model with CIES preferences and several modifications of this model by means of numerical solutions. One modification consists in the neoclassi-

---

[56] Maußner and Klump (1996, pp. 120/121) show that the IES for two immediate points in time equals the inverse of the elasticity of marginal utility.

cal model with Stone-Geary preferences. Easterly (1994) uses a constant-elasticity-of-substitution (CES) production function with the Jones-Manuelli property and Stone-Geary preferences to discuss the threshold effects of different policy measures on the long-run growth rates. Ben-David (1994) applies a neoclassical, exogenous growth framework extended by subsistence consumption to demonstrate the possibility of multiple balanced-growth equilibria. Similarly, Sarel (1994) studies a neoclassical growth model with an increasing intertemporal-elasticity-of-substitution (IES) function employing Stone-Geary preferences. Azariadis (1996) formulates a modified overlapping generations model with an endogenously determined subsistence level of consumption. Within this framework, it is shown that a poverty trap results if the fraction of subsistence consumption in GNP is sufficiently sensitive to past income whenever that income is within a critical range.[57] Finally, Ogaki, Ostry, and Reinhart (1996) show that the saving rate and its sensitivity to the interest rate is much higher in middle-income developing countries than in low-income developing countries within a linear growth model in which the IES rises with the level of wealth.[58] Despite its widespread use, the requirement of subsistence consumption has not yet been systematically applied to provide a potential explanation of the process of aggregate growth in DCs which is the aim of the chapter in hand.

3.3 A linear growth model with subsistence consumption

3.3.1 The model

The fundamental importance of the requirement of subsistence consumption for the process of growth mainly relevant to low-income countries is analysed. For this a linear one-sector growth model with Stone-Geary preferences is employed. The linear growth model can be described as linear in the sense that the time rate of change of the reproducible factor is linear in its level. More generally, in the case of models with more than one reproducible input, the time rate of change of each input is a constant-returns-to-scale function in the levels of input (Romer, 1989, p. 104). The linear growth model can be regarded as representing the basic version of a broad class of endogenous growth models including the Uzawa-Lucas

---

[57] This is one of three 'impatience traps' which are demonstrated within the overlapping generations framework (Azariadis, 1996, pp. 460).

[58] Ogaki, Ostry, and Reinhart (1996, pp. 60/61) only analyse balanced-growth equilibria though the main implications of the model concern the transition process to an asymptotic growth equilibrium.

model.[59] The notion of the requirement of subsistence consumption is formalised by the use of a Stone-Geary utility function. The economy considered is closed and the representative consumer-producer household is assumed to maximise its dynastic lifetime utility. The corresponding dynamic optimisation problem is a concave, infinite time problem of optimal control with a bounded control set:[60]

$$\max_{\{c(t)\}} \int_0^\infty \frac{[c(t) - \overline{c}]^{1-\theta} - 1}{1 - \theta} \cdot e^{-(\rho - n)t} \, dt$$

$$\text{s.t.} \quad \dot{k}(t) = (A - \delta - n)k(t) - c(t)$$

$$k(0) = k_0 \quad k(t) \geq 0$$

$$\overline{c} \leq c(t) \leq Ak(t).$$

$$(3.3)$$

All variables are expressed in per capita terms, t represents the time index, and a dot above a variable denotes its derivative with respect to time, i.e. $\dot{x}(t) \equiv dx(t)/dt$. The sole control variable is consumption, c, and the sole state variable is capital, k. Intertemporal preferences are described by the infinite sum of the discounted instantaneous utility, where $\overline{c}$ denotes the subsistence level of consumption, θ a constant preference parameter, ρ the individual time preference rate, and n the constant growth rate of population, respectively. As described above, the instantaneous utility function is strictly concave and possesses a variable elasticity of the marginal utility with respect to consumption, i.e. a variable IES. Gross output, y, is a linear function of capital, $y = Ak$, where A denotes a constant technology parameter. The absence of diminishing returns is crucial for the generation of endogenous growth and can be justified mainly by two interpretations: First, capital is thought to exhibit positive spill-over effects (Romer, 1986). Second, capital can be interpreted broadly as including human capital as well as physical capital (Rebelo, 1991).

---

[59] The linear growth model can be obtained from a Uzawa-Lucas economy that follows a balanced-growth path, has no externalities, and is characterised by identical technologies in the production of physical and human capital by aggregating both types of capital (Lucas, 1988 and Rebelo, 1992, p. 7). In addition, the linear model can be interpreted as the basic version of endogenous growth models which emphasises an increasing variety or quality of inputs (Pack, 1994, p. 56).

[60] For a presentation of optimal control theory with bounded control sets see Kamien and Schwartz (1981, Section 10). Especially for optimal control theory with state-dependent inequality constraints on the control variable see Feichtinger and Hartl (1986, Chapter 6).

In order to derive the first-order conditions for an optimal solution, the Lagrangian and current-value Hamiltonian for the dynamic problem (3.3) are set up (the time index is suppressed):

$$L(c,k,\lambda,v_1,v_2) = H(c,k,\lambda) + v_1(Ak - c) + v_2(c - \overline{c}) \tag{3.4}$$

$$H(c,k,\lambda) = \frac{(c - \overline{c})^{1-\theta} - 1}{1 - \theta} + \lambda[(A - \delta - n)k - c]. \tag{3.5}$$

The application of the maximum principle leads to the first-order conditions, where v_1 and v_2 denote the dynamic Lagrangian multipliers associated with each of the inequality constraints stated in (3.3):[61]

$$\frac{\partial L}{\partial \lambda} = \dot{k} = (A - \delta - n)k - c \tag{3.6}$$

$$\dot{\lambda} = \lambda(\rho - n) - \frac{\partial L}{\partial k} = \lambda(\rho + \delta - A) - v_1 A \tag{3.7}$$

$$\frac{\partial L}{\partial c} = (1 - \theta) \cdot (c - \overline{c})^{-\theta} - \lambda - v_1 + v_2 = 0 \tag{3.8}$$

$$v_1 \geq 0 \quad v_1(Ak - c) = 0 \tag{3.9}$$

$$v_2 \geq 0 \quad v_2(c - \overline{c}) = 0. \tag{3.10}$$

The first-order conditions (3.8), (3.9), and (3.10) indicate the basic possibility of corner and interior solutions: (i) A corner solution with the optimal choice of the control variable reaching its lower bound results if $(1 - \theta) \cdot (c - \overline{c})^{-\theta} \leq \lambda$. As long as the marginal utility falls short of the current-value shadow price of capital, a reduction of consumption to the lower bound of the control set is rational. The dynamic efficiency condition (3.7) indicates that this corner solution requires $A - \delta - \rho < 0$.[62] (ii) The optimal control reaches its upper bound provided that $(1 - \theta) \cdot (c - \overline{c})^{-\theta} \geq \lambda$. As long as the marginal utility exceeds the current-value shadow price of capital, an increase of consumption to the upper limit of the control set is rational. (iii) An interior solution is obtained for $(1 - \theta) \cdot (c - \overline{c})^{-\theta} = \lambda$, i.e. along the optimal path the marginal utility of consumption equals the current-value shadow price of capital.

---

[61] Because the Hamiltonian is concave in the control and the state, the necessary conditions are also sufficient for a maximum. In addition to the first-order conditions, an optimal trajectory must satisfy the transversality condition: $\lim_{t \to \infty} e^{-(\rho-n) \cdot t} \lambda(t)k(t) = 0$.

[62] The marginal utility approaches infinity as c approaches $\overline{c}$ and v_1 is zero for this corner solution.

The dynamics of consumption in the case of interior solutions can be obtained by differentiating $(c - \bar{c})^{-\theta} = \lambda$ with respect to time, subsequently dividing the result by the original relation, eliminating the shadow price using equation (3.7), and noting that v_1 is zero for interior solutions:

$$\frac{\dot{c}}{c} = \frac{c - \bar{c}}{\theta c} \cdot (A - \delta - \rho).$$

(3.11)

Equation (3.11) is the *Keynes-Ramsey rule* of optimal consumption in the case of a linear technology and Stone-Geary preferences. The first term on the right-hand side represents the variable IES. The IES reflects the ability as well as the willingness to substitute consumption over time.[63] The IES is determined by the constant preference parameter, θ, and the proportional difference between current consumption and the subsistence level of consumption. With a rising level of consumption, the IES increases and the individuals choose a steeper consumption path. In the case of unbounded growth, the IES eventually converges to a constant value θ^{-1}.

The differential equation (3.11) together with the equation of motion of capital stated in (3.3), i.e. $\dot{k}(t) = (A - \delta - n)k(t) - c(t)$, constitute the canonical equations of the dynamic problem. It represents an autonomous differential equation system that governs the dynamics of the economy for interior solutions.[64] An analytical solution to this linear first-order differential equation system can be easily found (see Appendix 3-1):

$$c(t) = \bar{c} + [c(0) - \bar{c}] \cdot e^{\theta^{-1}(A - \delta - \rho) \cdot t}$$

(3.12)

$$k(t) = \bar{k} + [k(0) - \bar{k}] \cdot e^{\theta^{-1}(A - \delta - \rho) \cdot t}$$

$$\text{with} \quad \bar{k} \equiv \frac{\bar{c}}{A - \delta - n} \quad \text{and} \quad A - \delta - n > 0 \,.\,{}^{65}$$

(3.13)

---

[63] Within the frame of the CIES-preference formulation the IES is usually interpreted as merely reflecting the willingness to substitute consumption intertemporally. As has been noted above, this turns out to represent a special case with $\bar{c} = 0$.

[64] The terminology is as follows: The differential equation system consisting in the control and the state variable is usually called the canonical system, while the differential equation system consisting in the state and the costate variable is called the Hamiltonian system of the dynamic problem (e.g. Gandolfo, 1996, p. 382 and Romer, 1989, p. 82).

[65] This parameter restriction is required in the course of the analytical solution; see Appendix 3-1.

3.3.2 Implications

3.3.2.1 Dynamic equilibria

Generically, there are two types of dynamic equilibria as immediately indicated by the solutions (3.12) and (3.13). On the one hand, there is the *subsistence steady state* $(\bar{c}, \bar{k})$, which eventually results whenever $A - \delta < \rho$. The individuals are simply not willing to postpone consumption because the net marginal product of capital is low relative to the time preference rate. The net saving rate (per capita) is zero and the output produced in each period just suffices to cover subsistence consumption and gross investment in order to replace the reduction in the stock of capital resulting from depreciation and population growth. Irrespective of the initial conditions, the subsistence steady state is the optimal long-run solution of the dynamic problem (3.3). In this case the subsistence steady state is saddle-point stable and can be termed as a low-level-development equilibrium.[66] On the other hand, an *asymptotic balanced-growth equilibrium* with consumption and capital growing asymptotically with constant rates of growth occurs if $A - \delta > \rho$. The economy pursues unbounded growth whenever the net marginal product of capital exceeds the time preference rate and the economy starts with an initial stock of capital above the subsistence level of capital. It is, however, impossible to catch up with richer countries and the process of convergence towards the asymptotic balanced-growth path might be extraordinarily long (see Section 3.3.3). The solutions (3.12) and (3.13) immediately show that the growth rates of consumption and capital approach their common asymptotic balanced-growth-equilibrium value as time converges to infinity (time index omitted):

$$\lim_{t \to \infty} \frac{\dot{c}}{c} = \lim_{t \to \infty} \frac{\dot{k}}{k} = \theta^{-1}(A - \delta - \rho). \tag{3.14}$$

For the special case that $A - \delta = \rho$ both dynamic equilibria collapse into a continuum of dynamic equilibria with zero growth, which are located along the ray $c = (A - \delta - n)k$. If the net marginal product of capital just equals the time preference rate the economy displays zero growth with consumption and capital probably above subsistence. In this case the realisation of one specific steady state is exclusively determined by the initial conditions. An external resource transfer would increase the level of consumption and capital but would not stimulate sustained growth. This situa-

---

[66] In contrast, a low-level-development trap or poverty trap requires that, for a given set of parameters, the economy possesses multiple dynamic equilibria. The lowest of these which is locally stable is called a poverty trap (Azariadis, 1996, pp. 450/451).

tion might be considered as merely representing a theoretical possibility which is not very probable. Nonetheless, this type of equilibrium with zero growth and consumption above subsistence will be worked out in a more plausible way in Section 3.4.

In addition, the solutions (3.12) and (3.13) allow the formulation of the stable arm of the saddle path in closed form, which is also called the policy function. The policy function shows the optimal choice of the control variable as a function of the state variable:[67]

$$c = z(k - \bar{k}) + \bar{c}, \quad \text{with} \quad z \equiv A - \delta - n - \theta^{-1}(A - \delta - \rho) > 0. \quad (3.15)$$

Given an initial condition for capital, the policy function immediately shows the corresponding value of consumption so that all necessary first-order conditions, including the transversality condition, are satisfied. In order to give a clear interpretation of all dynamic equilibria, the policy function is slightly reworded to:

$$c = (A - \delta - n)k - \theta^{-1}(A - \delta - \rho) \cdot (k - \bar{k}). \quad (3.16)$$

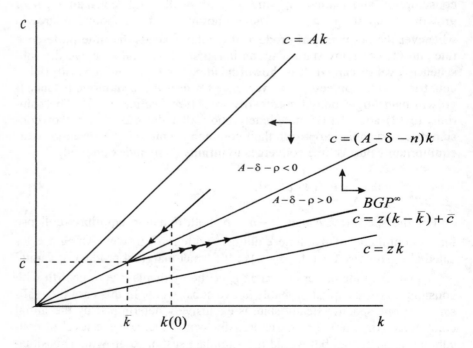

Fig. 3.1. Phase diagram of the linear growth model with Stone-Geary preferences

---

[67] For a description of the concept 'policy function' see Barro and Sala-i-Martin (1995, p. 76).

Equation (3.16) illustrates that consumption is chosen such that capital is constant, i.e. $\dot{k} = (A - \delta - n)k - c = 0$, whenever the capital stock equals its subsistence level or the net marginal product of capital equals the time preference rate. Fig. 3.1 shows the phase diagram of the linear growth model with Stone-Geary preferences, which illustrates the different dynamic equilibria depending on the constellation of parameters.

The three rays starting from the origin represent the production function, the $\dot{k} = 0$-locus, and the balanced-growth path of the linear growth model with CIES preferences, denoted as $c = zk$. The line starting at the subsistence steady state, ($\bar{c}, \bar{k}$), and running below the $\dot{k} = 0$-locus to the north-east is the asymptotic balanced-growth path of the linear growth model with Stone-Geary preferences, which is denoted as BGP^{∞}. Starting with an initial stock of capital above the subsistence level, $k(0) > \bar{k}$, Fig. 3.1 shows, in accordance with the policy function (3.16), three possibilities: (i) For $A - \delta - \rho < 0$ consumption is chosen above the $\dot{k} = 0$-locus and consequently the economy moves to the subsistence steady state. (ii) For $A - \delta - \rho = 0$ consumption is chosen to be located on the $\dot{k} = 0$-locus and the economy rests at the initial point. (iii) For $A - \delta - \rho > 0$ consumption is chosen below the $\dot{k} = 0$-locus and the starting point is located on the BGP^{∞}. This BGP^{∞} is linear and runs parallel to the balanced-growth path of the linear growth model with CIES preferences.[68] The arrows indicate the time dimension. In the case of the linear model with Stone-Geary preferences, the initial level of consumption exceeds that of the linear model with CIES preferences. Hence, less capital is accumulated in the case of the former economy and growth is taking place at a slower rate.

3.3.2.2 Transitional dynamics

In what follows, the transition process to an asymptotic balanced-growth equilibrium is investigated. In this case, the solutions (3.12) and (3.13) show that the growth rates of consumption and capital monotonically increase and eventually converge to their asymptotic balanced-growth values. The growth rate of income varies positively with the distance between the current state of the economy and the balanced-growth equilibrium. Consequently, the model illustrates a fundamental mechanism of (condi-

---

[68] However, the BGP^{∞} is not a ray starting at the origin and hence the c/k-ratio is not constant along this curve.

tional) ß-divergence: In the case of growth, the saving rate increases causing the growth rate of income to rise as well.

Using the policy function (3.16), the net saving rate per capita defined
as the relation between net investment and net output, i.e.
$s \equiv \left[(A - \delta - n)k - c\right]/\left[(A - \delta - n)k\right]$, reads as follows:

$$s = \frac{A - \delta - \rho}{\theta(A - \delta - n)} \cdot \frac{k - \bar{k}}{k}. \tag{3.17}$$

It should be noted explicitly that a value of the net saving rate equal to
zero implies a constant stock of capital. That is, the amount of gross output
not consumed (gross investment) just suffices to replace depreciation, δk,
and to enlarge the stock of capital in accordance with population growth,
nk. The preceding equation shows that the net saving rate is zero whenever the stock of capital equals its subsistence level. As far as the initial
capital stock exceeds its subsistence level, $k(0) > \bar{k}$, equation (3.17) demonstrates that the saving rate is positive whenever $A - \delta - \rho > 0$ and negative whenever $A - \delta - \rho < 0$. In both cases, the saving rate converges
monotonically to its dynamic-equilibrium value which reads

$$s^* = \frac{A - \delta - \rho}{\theta(A - \delta - n)} \text{ for } A - \delta - \rho > 0 \text{ and } s^* = 0 \text{ for } A - \delta - \rho < 0.$$

Growth theory, especially endogenous growth theory, as well as traditional development theory assign a dominant role to internal saving and
investment for the process of economic growth and development. Within
the latter, the saving rate is considered as being determined by the *ability
to save* as well as by the *willingness to save* (e.g. Hemmer, 1988, pp. 150).
These two concepts can be assigned directly to the determinants of the
saving rate as expressed in (3.17). The ability to save, which is also called
'economic or investible surplus', at any moment in time can be defined as
the proportional difference between the current and the subsistence level of
income. Within the framework of the linear growth model with subsistence
consumption, the ability to save is represented by the term $(k - \bar{k})/k$. It is
near zero for k near $\bar{k}$ and converges to unity as k approaches infinity.
Approximately the entire output is basically disposable for saving as capital grows without bound. The willingness to save, which is the second
determinant of the saving rate, is determined by the preference and technology parameters of the model as well as the growth rate of population
and is represented by the term $\dfrac{A - \delta - \rho}{\theta(A - \delta - n)}$. The subsequent Fig. 3.2

shows the time paths of the saving rate for different starting values of the stock of capital in relation to its subsistence level, i.e. for different initial abilities to save $a \equiv \dfrac{k(0) - \bar{k}}{k(0)}$, where the following set of parameters has been employed: $A = 0.1$, $\theta = 3$, $\delta = 0.02$, $\rho = 0.01$, $n = 0.03$, $\bar{c} = 2$. [69]

In the case of developed economies, a is sufficiently close to unity, so that the analysis of the requirement of subsistence consumption is nearly irrelevant for this group of countries. However, in the case of low-income countries the consideration of subsistence consumption might significantly influence the process of growth. The initial ability to save, as expressed by a, determines the saving rate chosen at the initial point in time and the subsequent time path, while the willingness to save determines the asymptotic value of the saving rate.

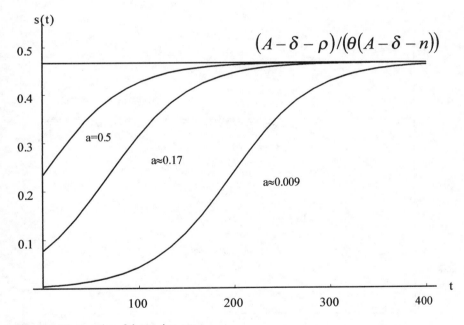

Fig. 3.2. Time paths of the saving rate

The rise in the saving and the investment rate causes the growth rate of capital to increase as well. The time path of the growth rate of capital, which equals the growth rate of income, increases monotonically and converges towards its asymptotic balanced-growth-equilibrium value as illustrated in Fig. 3.3. Obviously, the resulting time path of the growth rate of capital crucially depends on the initial stock of capital in relation to its subsistence level, a. The smaller this ratio, the longer it takes for the transition towards the asymptotic balanced-growth equilibrium. For $a \cong 0.009$, the growth rate of capital requires nearly 200 years to eliminate half the distance between its initial and its balanced-growth-equilibrium value. The time span required for the adjustment process is extremely long, and the implied rate of convergence is correspondingly small. This aspect is investigated in more detail within the next section.

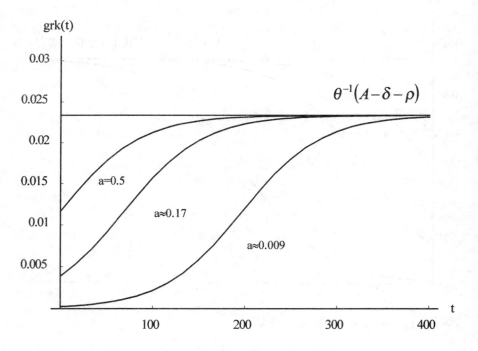

Fig. 3.3. Time paths of the growth rate of capital per capita

Despite its obvious simplicity, the linear growth model with subsistence consumption is extraordinarily useful because it is able to reproduce two of the stylised facts enumerated in the introduction, i.e. the positive correlation between the saving rate and the level of income [stylised fact (2)] and ß-divergence [stylised fact (3)]. In addition, the model displays important properties which are in line with theoretical and empirical research: (i) As Rebelo (1992) has pointed out, the model is able to explain internationally divergent growth dynamics even in the presence of international capital markets. (ii) The model avoids the counterfactual implication of extraordinarily high interest rates at early stages of economic development which characterises most versions of the neoclassical model (King and Rebelo, 1993). (iii) The model predicts that the IES is low for low (per capita) incomes and increases thereafter, which is in line with empirical research on the IES (Giovannini, 1985 and Ogaki, Ostry, and Reinhart, 1996). However, the model clearly fails to reproduce the hump-shaped relation between the growth rate and the level of income [stylised fact (4)]. In addition, provided that symmetry with respect to preference and technology parameters is supposed the model has difficulty in explaining the big diversity in growth rates for the group of low-income countries [stylised fact (1)].[70] More specifically, as far as divergent growth experiences are interpreted as transitional phenomena, the ability to explain these different growth rates depends essentially on the rate of convergence. This issue is investigated within the next section.

3.3.3 Convergence considerations

Within the context of convergence analyses as a branch of growth theory, two questions arise which are of fundamental interest for the process of growth and development: (i) Does the model imply convergence or divergence in the levels of per capita income between rich and poor economies? For poor countries to catch up with rich countries, it is necessary that the growth rate is higher compared to rich countries. This is the concept of absolute ß-convergence. Specifically, absolute ß-convergence is defined by a negative relation between the growth rate and the level of per capita income, i.e. poor countries grow faster on average than rich countries. If differences in the long-run growth rates are explicitly taken into account, the concept of conditional ß-convergence applies. Conditional ß-convergence requires that the growth rate of per capita income tends to be negatively related to the distance between the current state of the economy and its balanced-growth equilibrium.[71] Accordingly, (conditional) ß-

---

[70] These shortcomings will be taken up in Section 3.4.

[71] Conditional ß-convergence is a generic property of ordinary autonomous differential equations $\dot{x} = F(x)$ with a stationary equilibrium defined by $F(x^*) = 0$ and does not

divergence describes a positive relation between the growth rate of per capita income and the distance between the current state of the economy and the balanced-growth equilibrium. In this case, the difference in the levels of per capita income between rich and poor countries grows without bound.[72] (ii) What does the model predict about the rate of convergence towards its (probably asymptotic) balanced-growth equilibrium? This second question is meaningful irrespective of the answer to the first question and concerns the quantitative implications of the transition process.[73] The rate of convergence provides important information about whether the

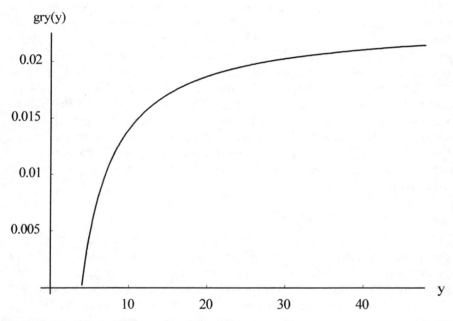

Fig. 3.4. Subsistence-divergence mechanism

---

depend on the specific functional form of the differential equations (Koch, 1997, pp. 2/3). The convergence issue is discussed comprehensively in Section 5.

[72] Most growth models imply conditional ß-convergence like the Solow-Swan as well as the Ramsey-Cass-Koopmans model (e.g. Barro and Sala-i-Martin, 1995, pp. 36 and pp. 80). An example for a growth model with ß-divergence is Romer (1986).

[73] A model might contain the qualitative implication of a positive relation between the growth rate and the level of per capita income (ß-divergence) during the transition to the balanced-growth equilibrium. At the same time it is meaningful to ask how fast it converges to its balanced-growth equilibrium.

emphasis of analysis should be placed on transitional or balanced-growth dynamics. In addition, beside the qualitative implication of ß-convergence or ß-divergence, the rate of convergence is an important quantitative property of each model which represents an empirically refutable hypothesis.[74]

The linear growth model with subsistence consumption implies *conditional ß-divergence*. The growth rate of per capita income increases with the level of per capita income conditioned on the balanced-growth equilibrium or − in the terminology of econometrics − after controlling for the influence of those variables which determine the long-run growth rate. Fig. 3.4 plots the relation between the growth rate, $gry(y)$, and the level of per capita income, y, based on the same set of parameters used within the preceding section with $a \cong 0.009$.

The reason for this divergence mechanism, which might in analogy to the neoclassical convergence mechanism be labelled as '*subsistence-divergence mechanism*', is simply that in the case of growth the ability to save rises continuously. Consequently, the saving and investment rates increase as well. Unlike the neoclassical model, the linear growth model displays a constant marginal and average product of capital. As a result, the productive contribution of the entire stock of the reproducible factors remains constant and an increase in the investment rate fully translates into an increase in the growth rate of output.

In the next step consider the quantitative implications of the transition process. For this, the current state of the economy is expressed in terms of a variable $x(t)$ so that this variable converges monotonically to a stationary value denoted by $x*$, which represents the balanced-growth equilibrium of the economy. The *instantaneous speed or rate of convergence* can reasonably be defined as (the negative of) that share of the distance between the current state of the economy and its balanced-growth equilibrium which is eliminated during the current period (Romer, 1996, p. 21 and Ortigueira and Santos, 1997, p. 390):

$$\lambda(t) \equiv -\frac{\dot{x}(t)}{x(t) - x*}. \tag{3.18}$$

The instantaneous rate of convergence shown in (3.18) is only constant if the underlying differential equation $\dot{x}(t) = F[x(t)]$ is linear. For non-linear differential equations, the rate of convergence varies with the dis-

---

[74] For example, Mankiw, Romer, and Weil (1992) demonstrate that the neoclassical growth model is quantitatively consistent with the empirical estimates of the rate of convergence if it is extended to explicitly include human capital. In addition, for this see Barro and Sala-i-Martin (1995, Chapter 3) and Klenow and Rodríguez-Clare (1997, p. 604).

tance $x(t) - x*$.[75] Because the economy in question exhibits unbounded growth, the distance between the current state of the economy and its balanced-growth equilibrium, $x(t) - x*$, cannot be expressed in terms of the original variables, i.e. consumption per capita or capital per capita. This distance must rather be expressed in terms of variables which are functions of the original variables and converge, at least asymptotically, to stationary values. This is true, for example, for the growth rate of capital per capita as well as the consumption-capital ratio.

The instantaneous rate of convergence for the linear growth model with Stone-Geary preferences is expressed on the basis of the consumption-capital ratio.[76] For this, both the c/k-ratio and the logarithm of the c/k-ratio are employed. Both variables move monotonically to their stationary value, which reads $A - \delta - n - \theta^{-1}(A - \delta - \rho)$ in the case of the c/k-ratio and $\ln\left[A - \delta - n - \theta^{-1}(A - \delta - \rho)\right]$ in the case of the logarithm of the c/k-ratio. The rate of convergence calculated on the basis of the c/k-ratio shows the instantaneous as well as the 'true' rate of convergence. This rate of convergence is true in the sense that it describes the actual rate of convergence of the economy expressed in original variables.[77] However, empirical estimates on the rate of convergence are usually based on logarithmic variables. Therefore, the logarithm of the c/k-ratio is additionally employed in order to obtain a perfect comparability between the theoretically implied and the empirically estimated values of the rate of convergence.

The asymptotic value of the rate of convergence amounts to 2.3 per cent. However, Fig. 3.5 demonstrates that the rate of convergence locally around the asymptotic balanced-growth equilibrium is not a good estimate

---

[75] Because the differential equations which describe the dynamics of the economy are mostly non-linear, the rate of convergence is usually calculated on the basis of a first-order Taylor series approximation around a stationary value and is therefore only valid within a 'small neighbourhood' around the stationary value (Barro and Sala-i-Martin, 1995, pp. 36/37 and Romer, 1996, pp. 21/22). For a method which allows the calculation of the instantaneous rate of convergence without having the solution of the differential equation under study see Koch (1997, pp. 6/7).

[76] The differential equation of this variable is non-linear. Consequently, the instantaneous rate of convergence varies in the course of economic development.

[77] Ortigueira and Santos (1997, p. 383) state that generically along the stable path to the balanced-growth equilibrium all endogenous variables must converge with the same rate. Within the frame of the Uzawa-Lucas model they use the time allocation variable to determine the rate of convergence.

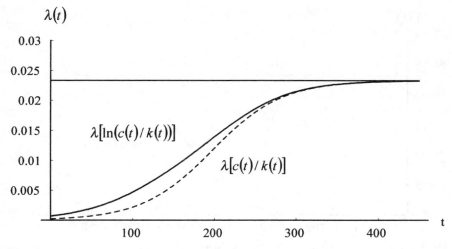

Fig. 3.5. The instantaneous rate of convergence

for the global converging behaviour.[78] At early stages of economic development, the rate of convergence is extraordinarily low (below 0.1 per cent
per year at the initial point in time) and increases only slightly. As a result,
the time span required for the transition process towards the asymptotic
balanced-growth equilibrium is extremely long. As demonstrated above,
the saving rate and the growth rate of capital per capita require a very long
time span for the transition towards their balanced-growth-equilibrium
values with half-life times of about 200 years. The economy converges
asymptotically at a constant rate towards its asymptotic balanced-growth
equilibrium, i.e. the rate of convergence is asymptotically constant either.

Moreover, it should be noted that the initial value and the time path of
the instantaneous rate of convergence appear to dependend crucially on the
initial distance from the subsistence steady state.

Fig. **3.6** shows the time path of the instantaneous rate of convergence in
the case that the economy starts 'extremely close' to subsistence; the initial
ability to save amounts to $a \approx 0.00001$.[79] The instantaneous rate of convergence stays nearly constant for a considerable time period of about 250
years; in fact, it increases very slowly. In summary, the big diversity in
growth rates [stylised fact (1)] can partly be explained to represent a transition phenomenon.

---

[78] In contrast, Ortigueira and Santos (1997, pp. 390/391) demonstrate that the local rate of
convergence around the dynamic equilibrium is a good estimate for the global convergence
behaviour within a wide range of capital per capita in the case of the neoclassical and the
Uzawa-Lucas model.

[79] This low initial endowment with productive resources might be the result of a war or a
natural catastrophe, for example.

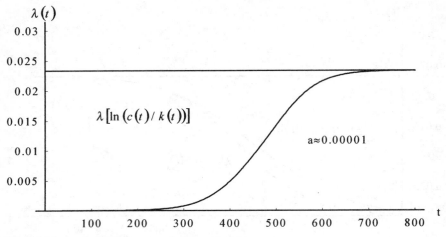

Fig. 3.6. The rate of convergence close to subsistence

However, if international symmetry with respect to preferences and technology is supposed, the range of possible growth rate differences is restricted.[80]

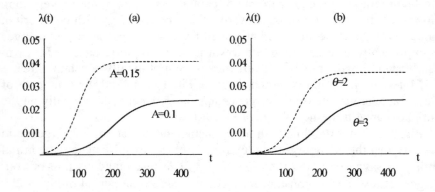

Fig. 3.7. Instantaneous rate of convergence – comparative dynamics

---

[80] This can be illustrated as follows: Define a DC as an economy with income per capita of $y*$ or less, then the range of possible growth rates of per capita income which can be explained by the model in hand varies from 0 to $gry(y*)$.

Finally, Fig. 3.7 shows the time paths of the instantaneous rate of convergence based on the c/k-ratio for alternative parametrisations of the marginal product of capital, A, and the elasticity of the marginal utility, θ. In general, each variation of parameters which increases the growth rate of income per capita results in a reduction of the time span required for the transition process. As a result, the rate of convergence increases. According to Fig. 3.7 (a), the rate of convergence increases with the (marginal and average) productivity of capital. A rise in the (marginal) rate of return to capital increases the willingness to save. In addition, a rise in the average product of capital increases the productive contributions of capital to output growth and reduces the time span required for the adjustment process to the balanced-growth equilibrium.

Fig. 3.7 (b) displays a negative relation between the rate of convergence and the elasticity of the marginal utility. A falling elasticity of marginal utility, i.e. a rising IES, increases the willingness to save. The saving rate decreases causing the growth rate of income to decrease as well. As a result, growth increases, the time span for transition shortens, and the rate of convergence rises.

3.4 Extensions of the basic linear growth model

The linear growth model discussed in the previous section is able to reproduce the positive correlation between the saving rate and the level of per capita income [stylised fact (2)] as well as ß-divergence [stylised fact (3)]. However, supposing that the symmetry assumption applies, the model has difficulty in explaining the big diversity in growth rates [stylised fact (1)] and it clearly fails to reproduce the hump-shaped pattern of growth [stylised fact (4)]. Consequently, the basic model will be extended in order to provide a potential explanation for the remaining empirical regularities.

3.4.1 The model

The basic linear growth model with Stone-Geary preferences is extended in two directions. First, the presence of fixed factors such as land or (raw) labour causes the production function to exhibit diminishing returns to the reproducible factor. The marginal product of these factors is, however, regarded as being bounded from below, i.e. the production function is represented by a Jones-Manuelli technology. Second, in order to capture the influence of national government policy, a general index reflecting several distortions is incorporated into the production function. The aggregate production function of the private sector for gross output 'net of distortions' is assumed to read as follows:

$$y(t) = (1 - \tau) \cdot \left[Ak(t) + Bk(t)^\alpha \right],$$
(3.19)

where A, B, and α (with $0 < \alpha < 1$) denote constant technology parameters and y denotes gross output. The distortions summarised in τ, with $0 \leq \tau < 1$, reduce the marginal product of the reproducible factors and can be considered as resulting mainly from bad government policies which are frequently found especially in DCs. The extent of distortions is considered as varying internationally and results from income or investment taxes (Barro, 1990; Jones and Manuelli, 1990; and Rebelo, 1991, 1992),[81] inflation taxes (Easterly, King, Levine, and Rebelo, 1992 and Easterly, 1994), bad institutional set-ups (North, 1987 and Rebelo, 1992), sectoral distortions due to unequal taxation of different sectors, dual exchange rate systems, and sectorally discriminating tariffs and import quotas (Easterly, King, Levine, and Rebelo, 1992; Rebelo, 1992; and Easterly, 1994). The production function (3.19) exhibits the Jones-Manuelli property, i.e. the marginal product of the reproducible factors decreases, however, converging to a positive constant as capital grows without bound:

$\lim\limits_{k \to \infty} \dfrac{\partial y}{\partial k} = (1 - \tau)A > 0$ (Jones and Manuelli, 1990, pp. 1016/1017; Jones

and Manuelli, 1997, pp. 81/82; and Easterly, 1994, pp. 525).[82]

The model with subsistence consumption and a Jones-Manuelli technology including a general index of distortions reads as follows; as before all variables are expressed in per capita terms:

$$\max_{\{c(t)\}} \int_0^\infty \frac{[c(t) - \overline{c}]^{1-\theta} - 1}{1 - \theta} \cdot e^{-(\rho - n) \cdot t} \, dt$$

s.t. $\dot{k}(t) = (1 - \tau) \cdot \left[Ak(t) + Bk(t)^\alpha \right] - (\delta + n)k(t) - c(t)$

$k(0) = k_0 \qquad k(t) \geq 0$

$\overline{c} \leq c(t) \leq (1 - \tau) \cdot \left[Ak(t) + Bk(t)^\alpha \right].$
(3.20)

---

[81] As far as taxes reduce the rate of return to reproducible inputs they lower the rate of growth. However, in order to determine the overall effects on growth and welfare the use of tax revenues is crucial. If tax revenues are 'thrown away', growth and welfare decrease. If tax revenues finance public consumption, and public consumption enters the utility function, growth decreases but welfare does not necessarily fall (Rebelo, 1992, pp. 10/11). If tax revenues finance public goods which are inputs in production, the effect on growth and welfare is unequivocal (Barro, 1990).

[82] The Jones-Manuelli property also applies for a CES function with two inputs and an elasticity of substitution greater than unity (Easterly, 1994, p. 529 and Jones and Manuelli, 1997, p. 82).

The current-value Hamiltonian for the dynamic optimisation problem (3.20) in the case of interior solutions accordingly reads (the time index is omitted):

$$H(c,k,\lambda) = \frac{(c-\bar{c})^{1-\theta} - 1}{1-\theta} + \lambda\left[(1-\tau)\cdot\left(Ak + Bk^{\alpha}\right) - (\delta+n)k - c\right], \quad (3.21)$$

and the necessary first-order conditions are: [83]

$$\frac{\partial H}{\partial \lambda} = \dot{k} = (1-\tau)\cdot\left(Ak + Bk^{\alpha}\right) - (\delta+n)k - c \qquad (3.22)$$

$$\dot{\lambda} = \lambda(\rho-n) - \frac{\partial H}{\partial k} = \lambda\left[\rho + \delta - (1-\tau)\cdot\left(A + \alpha Bk^{\alpha-1}\right)\right] \qquad (3.23)$$

$$\frac{\partial H}{\partial c} = (1-\theta)\cdot(c-\bar{c})^{-\theta} - \lambda = 0. \qquad (3.24)$$

Differentiating (3.24) with respect to time, subsequently dividing by the original relation, and eliminating the shadow price using (3.23) yields the optimal growth rate of consumption per capita:

$$\frac{\dot{c}}{c} = \frac{c-\bar{c}}{c\theta}\cdot\left[(1-\tau)\cdot\left(A + \alpha Bk^{\alpha-1}\right) - \delta - \rho\right]. \qquad (3.25)$$

The preceding equation shows the Keynes-Ramsey rule of optimal consumption. Similarly to the linear growth model with Stone-Geary preferences, the first term on the right-hand side represents the IES, while the second term shows the difference between the net marginal product of capital and the time preference rate. Equation (3.25) indicates the possibility of different dynamic equilibria which are investigated within the next section. In addition, in the case of growth there are two opposing forces affecting the evolution of the growth rate of consumption. Therefore, it is unequivocal *a priori* whether the growth rate increases or decreases. The simulation results presented in Section 4.2.2 illustrate the transitional dynamics at least for a specific set of parameter values.

---

[83] Because the Hamiltonian is concave in the control and the state variable, the necessary conditions are also sufficient for a maximum. In addition to the first-order conditions, an optimal trajectory must satisfy the transversality condition: $\lim\limits_{t\to\infty} e^{-(\rho-n)\cdot t}\lambda(t)k(t) = 0$.

3.4.2 Implications

3.4.2.1 Dynamic equilibria

In order to discuss the implications of the model, the canonical equations of the dynamic problem (3.20) are considered. This autonomous differential equation system governs the dynamics of the economy in the case of interior solutions:

$$\dot{c} = (c - \bar{c})\theta^{-1}\left[(1-\tau)\cdot\left(A + \alpha B k^{\alpha-1}\right) - \delta - \rho\right] \qquad (3.26)$$

$$\dot{k} = (1-\tau)\cdot\left(Ak + Bk^{\alpha}\right) - (\delta + n)k - c . \qquad (3.27)$$

There are three dynamic equilibria defined by constant growth rates. Specifically, the model displays two steady states with stationary values of consumption and capital and one balanced-growth equilibrium with unbounded growth. With respect to (3.26) it is clear that there are three possibilities for the long-run evolution of consumption: (i) zero growth with consumption at subsistence [$\dot{c} = 0$, $c^* = \bar{c}$]; (ii) zero growth with consumption above subsistence [$\dot{c} = 0$, $c^* > \bar{c}$]; and (iii) unbounded growth [$c \to \infty$]. All three possibilities will be discussed in more detail.

The subsistence equilibrium with zero growth and consumption at subsistence can be the result of two constellations: (i) the initial consumption equals its subsistence level, $c(0) = \bar{c}$, the ability to save is zero, and the economy rests in a low-level equilibrium, not necessarily stable. (ii) The private net marginal product of capital evaluated at the subsistence capital stock falls short of the time preference rate, i.e.
$(1-\tau)\cdot\left(A + \alpha B \bar{k}^{\alpha-1}\right) - \delta - \rho < 0$. As a result of the diminishing marginal returns to capital, the validity of the preceding inequality evaluated at the subsistence level of capital implies that this inequality holds for each initial stock of capital above subsistence. In this case, individuals are simply not willing to postpone consumption. The individuals will consider it optimal to reduce the stock of capital and accept a decreasing level of consumption eventually converging to the subsistence equilibrium ($\bar{c}, \bar{k}$). The steady-state value of capital is implicitly defined by
$(1-\tau)\cdot\left(A\bar{k} + B\bar{k}^{\alpha}\right) - (\delta + n)\bar{k} - \bar{c} = 0$.[84] The subsistence steady state is (locally) saddle-point stable provided that the net marginal product of capital at subsistence exceeds the rate of population growth (see Appendix 3-4).

---

[84] This equation might have two solutions for $\bar{k}$; one less than the golden-rule value for k and one greater. In this case, the lower value is the relevant one (Easterly, 1994, p. 531).

The second steady state with consumption above subsistence applies whenever the private net marginal product of the capital exceeds the time preference rate at the initial point in time, i.e.

$(1-\tau)\cdot\left[A+\alpha Bk(0)^{\alpha-1}\right]-\delta-\rho>0$ with $k(0)>\overline{k}$. In this case, the individuals are able and willing to substitute consumption intertemporally and the growth rate of consumption is positive. However, as the economy grows the private marginal product of capital eventually converges to a constant. This asymptotic marginal product of capital might be too low in order to guarantee unbounded growth: $(1-\tau)A-\delta-\rho\leq0$. Eventually the golden rule will apply, i.e. the private net marginal product of capital equals the time preference rate and the economy converges to the golden

rule steady state with $k^*=\left(\dfrac{\delta+\rho-(1-\tau)A}{(1-\tau)\alpha B}\right)^{\frac{1}{\alpha-1}}$ and

$c^*=\left[(1-\tau)A-(\delta+n)\right]k^*+Bk^{*\alpha}$. Again, this steady state is (locally) saddle-point stable as shown in Appendix 3-4.

The asymptotic balanced-growth equilibrium applies whenever the economy starts with productive resources above the subsistence level and, more importantly, if the growth condition is initially and even asymptotically valid: $(1-\tau)A-\delta-\rho>0$. In this case, the economy pursues unbounded growth. From (3.26) one can see that the asymptotic growth rate of consumption reads: $\lim\limits_{t\to\infty}\dfrac{\dot{c}}{c}=\theta^{-1}\left[(1-\tau)A-\delta-\rho\right]$. In addition, equation (3.27) indicates that consumption and capital must expand asymptotically at the same rate if the growth rate of capital should converge asymptotically to a constant value:[85]

$$\lim_{t\to\infty}\frac{\dot{c}}{c}=\lim_{t\to\infty}\frac{\dot{k}}{k}=\theta^{-1}\left[(1-\tau)A-\delta-\rho\right]. \tag{3.28}$$

Within the c/k-plane, the asymptotic balanced-growth path, BGP^∞, converges to a ray starting from the origin. This ray describes the asymptotic direction of the BGP^∞.

Provided that the economy starts above the subsistence steady state, the resulting long-run equilibrium is independent from the initial condition. However, the lower bound of the private rate of return to the reproducible inputs in relation to the time preference rate crucially determines whether the economy stagnates or pursues unbounded growth. As has been shown

---

[85] See Barro and Sala-i-Martin (1995, pp. 161) for a similar reasoning within the context of the Jones-Manuelli model with CIES preferences.

in the literature, the private rate of return is primarily affected by government policies, which were summarised by the index of overall distortions. Consequently, international differences in detrimental government policies which reduce the marginal product of reproducible factors represent a potential explanation of internationally diverging growth experiences. Therefore, the incorporation of an index of distortions into the production function enables a meaningful 'explanation' of different long-run as well as different transitional growth rates while assuming symmetry with respect to preferences and technology between the economy under study and the rest of the world (Easterly, King, Levine, and Rebelo, 1992; Rebelo, 1992; and Easterly, 1994).[86]

3.4.2.2 Transitional dynamics: simulation results

In order to illustrate the dynamics of the Jones-Manuelli model with subsistence consumption, the transition process in the case of unbounded growth is simulated. This signifies that the system of differential equations (3.26) and (3.27) is approximated numerically, supposing that the growth condition, $(1 - \tau)A - \delta - \rho > 0$, holds. This is done by means of the subroutine NDSolve of Mathematica®. As has been noted above, the growth model under study belongs to the class of growth models which don't possess a balanced-growth equilibrium. Nevertheless, it possesses an asymptotic balanced-growth path, BGP^{∞}, which converges to a ray starting from the origin. This ray describes the asymptotic direction of the BGP^{∞}. It is unique and saddle-point stable (see Appendix 3-4).[87] The following set of parameters is employed: $\tau = 0.1$, $A = 0.1$, $B = 0.1$, $\alpha = 0.8$, $\delta = 0.02$, $n = 0.03$, $\theta = 1$, $\rho = 0.05$, and $\overline{c} = 2$.[88]

---

[86] At this general level, the 'explanation' outlined above has no empirical content because it does not bear any refutable hypothesis. Nonetheless, it demonstrates that static distortions, which lower the marginal product of those factors that can be accumulated, have dynamic effects in the sense that they lower the long-run growth rate.

[87] Further models with the property of asymptotic balanced growth are the linear growth model with Stone-Geary preferences (see Section 3.3), the Jones-Manuelli model (Jones and Manuelli, 1990), and growth models with productive consumption (see Chapter 4).

[88] The initial conditions are expressed by the parameter $a \cong 0.00003$ and were determined as follows: First, an arbitrarily but sufficiently high value of capital per capita is selected. The value of consumption is chosen to be located on the ray which describes the asymptotic direction of the BGP^{∞}. Second, starting from this point the dynamic system is solved backwards; the resulting trajectory runs into the point $(\overline{c}, \overline{k})$. Third, the starting point of the forward solution is chosen to be located on this trajectory slightly above $(\overline{c}, \overline{k})$. The initial values of the backward solution are sufficiently high in the following

The most important difference between the linear growth model with Stone-Geary preferences and the Jones-Manuelli model with Stone-Geary preferences concerns the possibility to reproduce *non-monotonic dynamics of growth rates*. Intuitively, the equation for the growth rate of consumption (3.25) indicates that there are two opposing forces governing the dynamics of growth rates. At early stages of economic development, the IES is low reflecting a low ability to save due to the requirement of subsistence considerations. As the economy develops, the subsistence-divergence mechanism causes the saving rate and the growth rate of output to increase. On the other hand, the Jones-Manuelli technology (3.19) exhibits a falling marginal product of capital. As a result, the neoclassical convergence mechanism causes the growth rate of income to fall. For specific parametrisations the interaction of both forces can produce a non-monotonic pattern of growth rate dynamics.

Fig. 3.8 shows the time paths of the intertemporal elasticity of substitution, $IES(t)$, the marginal product of capital, $mpc(t)$, the saving rate, $s(t)$, the consumption-capital ratio, $c(t)/k(t)$, the growth rate of income, $gry(t)$, and the relation between the growth rate of income and the logarithm of income, $gry(\ln y)$, respectively. Several observations appear worth being discussed.

The growth rate of income displays non-monotonic dynamics; specifically a *hump-shaped pattern* occurs. Fig. 3.8 (e) shows the time-path of the growth rate of income, while Fig. 3.8 (f) shows the relation between the growth rate of income and the logarithm of income. Growth accelerates initially reaching a maximum growth rate and decelerates subsequently. In other words, the model implies conditional ß-divergence for the lower range of income and conditional ß-convergence for the higher range of income. Eventually, the growth rate converges towards its asymptotic balanced-growth-equilibrium value. The Jones-Manuelli model with subsistence consumption is therefore able to reproduce an important stylised fact of economic growth [stylised fact (4)].[89] This pattern of evolution is the result of two opposing forces as can be illustrated on the basis of the simulation results: First, at early stages of economic development the IES increases [Fig. 3.8 (a)] reflecting an increase in the ability to save. As a result, the saving rate rises initially [Fig. 3.8 (c)], causing the growth rate of income to rise as well; the subsistence-divergence mechanism. Second,

---

sense: Multiplying these values by two and following the same procedure does not alter the time paths as shown in Fig. 3.8 visually.

[89] It should be noted explicitly that this result essentially hinges on the value of the parameter α. If this technology parameter is reduced sufficiently, the marginal product of capital decreases more rapidly. As a result, a monotonic rise in the growth rate of income occurs.

the marginal product of capital falls with an increase in the level of capital [Fig. 3.8 (b)]. Economically, this bears two implications: (i) A fall in the rate of return to the factors that can be accumulated reduces the incentives to save.[90] (ii) Along with the marginal product the average product of capital decreases as well. Consequently, the productive contribution of the whole stock of capital to output growth is reduced and the growth rate of output falls. Both mechanisms together [(i) and (ii)] constitute the neoclassical convergence mechanism. In the present case, the subsistence-divergence mechanism dominates the neoclassical convergence mechanism at early stages of economic development, while the reverse is true for later stages of development.

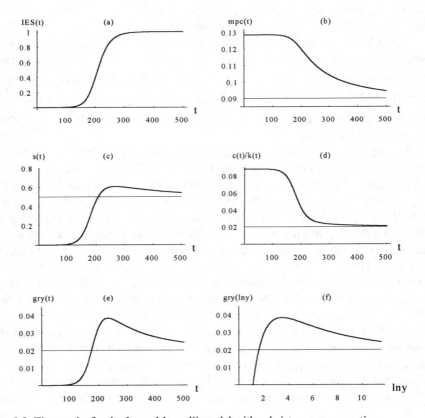

Fig. 3.8. Time paths for the Jones-Manuelli model with subsistence consumption

---

[90] The interaction of this mechanism together with the increase of the saving rate as a result of a rise in the ability to save explains the slight overshooting of the saving rate [Fig. 3.8 (c)].

The c/k-ratio falls monotonically and converges towards its asymptotic balanced-growth-equilibrium value [Fig. 3.8 (d)]. Therefore, the c/k-ratio is used to give a rough estimate of the *average rate of convergence*. Analogous to the definition of the instantaneous rate of convergence used in the previous section, the average rate of convergence during any time interval $[t, t+\upsilon]$ can be defined as (the negative of) the average share of the difference between the current state of the economy and its balanced-growth equilibrium which is eliminated during the time interval under consideration, i.e. $\lambda_a(t,t+\upsilon) \equiv -\dfrac{[x(t+\upsilon)-x(t)]/\upsilon}{x(t)-x^*}$. The average rate of convergence for $t = 0$ and $\upsilon = 200$ measured on the basis of the c/k-ratio reads accordingly: $\lambda_a(0,200) = -\dfrac{[x(200)-x(0)]/200}{x(0)-x^*} \cong 0.0034$.

That is, during the first 200 years on average 0.34 per cent of the distance between the initial state of the economy and the balanced-growth-equilibrium gets eliminated per year. As in the model of the previous section, this value is extraordinarily low and the implied time span required for the transition to the balanced-growth equilibrium is extremely long.[91]

At last, the following observation is worth noting. The previous Fig. 3.8 shows that the saving rate [Fig. 3.8 (c)] and the growth rate of income [Fig. 3.8 (e)] seem to be nearly constant during the first 100 years; in fact they increase very slowly. Empirically, this pattern of dynamics could be interpreted as representing a balanced-growth equilibrium with low saving and low growth. However, in the present case this pattern of dynamics represents a transitional phenomenon. Following this early stage of economic development, saving and growth increase significantly. This pattern of dynamics is consistent with several theoretical approaches as well as empirical observations on the stages of economic development. As an example, Reynolds (1983) comprehensively describes the growth experiences of the 'third world' over the time period from 1850 to 1980. He stresses the distinction between extensive and intensive growth.[92] According to Reynolds, most countries experienced a turning point, i.e. extensive turned into intensive growth. Within the frame of the present model, this 'turning point' occurs after about 100 years as Fig. 3.8 (e) indicates. Therefore, the growth model under study is able to explain this transition from extensive

---

[91] The possibility of a non-monotonic relation between the growth rate and the level of per capita income casts some doubt on the usual procedure to estimate the rate of convergence.

[92] Extensive growth is defined as population growth with per capita income being constant, while intensive growth is defined as population growth with a rise in per capita income (Reynolds, 1983, p. 943).

to intensive growth endogenously.[93] However, the implication of a smoothly increasing growth rate can be questioned on empirical grounds. Pritchett (1998), for example, reveals a high instability in growth rates which is especially marked for DCs. This finding does not necessarily contradict the models presented in this chapter. The models are compatible with single or infrequently occurring large permanent shocks.[94] In this case the time path of the growth rate of income would show a discontinuity. Provided that the shocks are uncorrelated across countries the average pattern of growth appears nonetheless consistent with the transitional dynamics described above.

3.5 Summary and conclusion

The requirement of subsistence consumption unambiguously affects the process of economic growth. It clearly restricts the ability to save not only for levels of per capita income at or slightly above subsistence. The intertemporal elasticity of substitution, which reflects both the ability and the willingness to save, increases with the level of per capita consumption and converges asymptotically to a constant. As a result, the requirement of subsistence consumption causes the growth rate of income to increase. It therefore represents an important mechanism of ß-divergence, which might be called subsistence-divergence mechanism.[95] For realistic and widely employed parameter values, the rate of convergence is exceptionally low at early stages of economic development and the time span required for the transition towards the asymptotic balanced-growth equilibrium is correspondingly long.

Despite its obvious simplicity the linear growth model with subsistence consumption is able to reproduce two of the stylised facts enumerated in the introduction, which primarily apply to the lower range of per capita income. The model implies a rise in the saving rate along with the level of per capita income [stylised fact (2)] as well as ß-divergence [stylised fact

---

[93] Reynolds' (1983) concept of 'turning point' resembles the take-off period originated by Rostow (1956).

[94] Balke and Fomby (1991) show that the empirical evidence is compatible with time series models which allow for large, infrequent permanent shocks like wars, earthquakes, financial crises, 'technological breakthroughs'. Sarel (1994), for example, views 'development' as the transition from a 'traditional period' with no technical progress to a 'modern period' with a positive rate of technical progress. In accordance with this view, he assumes that the rate of technical progress shows a discrete jump.

[95] The growth dynamics of the real world are simultaneously affected by different mechanisms of convergence and divergence. Several authors have proposed to separate the different mechanisms of convergence (Barro and Sala-i-Martin, 1992, p. 247 and de la Fuente, 1997, p. 69).

(3)]. On account of the extraordinarily low values of the rate of convergence at early stages of economic development, different growth rates can partly be explained to represent transitional phenomena [stylised fact (1)]. However, if international symmetry with respect to preferences and technology is supposed, the possible range of growth rates is restricted. Hence, the linear growth model with subsistence consumption has some difficulty in explaining the big diversity in growth experiences observable for the group of developing countries. In addition, the model clearly fails to reproduce the hump-shaped pattern of growth [stylised fact (4)].

An extension of the basic model by a general index of policy-induced distortions, which is sensibly allowed to vary internationally, and by diminishing marginal returns to the factors that can be accumulated permits a more satisfactory explanation of stylised fact (1). The incorporation of a general index of distortions enhances the possible range of long-run growth rates while maintaining symmetry with respect to preferences and technology. The considerable diversity in growth rates is explained to result from both transitional dynamics and different balanced-growth equilibria. The extended model shows two steady states and one asymptotic balanced-growth equilibrium. The selection of the dynamic equilibrium depends crucially on the relation between the marginal product of capital net of depreciation as well as 'net of distortions' on the one hand and the time preference rate on the other. In the case of unbounded growth one observes policy continuity, i.e. the growth rate falls steadily as the extent of distortions increases (Easterly, 1994, p. 532 and Jones and Manuelli, 1997, pp. 86/87). Altogether, policy-induced distortions are important for understanding the big diversity in growth rates [stylised fact (1)].

Finally, the extended model enables a potential explanation of the remaining stylised fact. The interaction between the subsistence-divergence mechanism and the neoclassical convergence mechanism produces an acceleration of growth subsequently followed by a deceleration, i.e. the hump-shaped relation between the growth rate and the level of per capita income [stylised fact (4)].

3.6 Appendix

3.6.1 The linear growth model with subsistence consumption

Appendix 3-1: Analytical solution

The first-order conditions of the dynamic problem (3.3) lead to the linear system of differential equations in the control and the state variable:

$$\dot{c}(t) = c(t)\theta^{-1}(A - \delta - \rho) - \bar{c}\theta^{-1}(A - \delta - \rho) \qquad \text{(A.3.1)}$$

$$\dot{k}(t) = (A - \delta - n)k(t) - c(t). \qquad \text{(A.3.2)}$$

Because of the linear technology the differential equation system can be solved one for one. The solution to (A.3.1) is (e.g. Gandolfo, 1996, Chapter 12):

$$c(t) = \bar{c} + b_1 e^{\theta^{-1}(A - \delta - \rho)t}, \qquad \text{(A.3.3)}$$

where b_1 is a constant of integration which must be chosen optimally in order to satisfy the transversality condition. The linear first-order differential equation in k accordingly reads:

$$\dot{k}(t) = (A - \delta - n)k(t) - \bar{c} - b_1 e^{\theta^{-1}(A - \delta - \rho)t}. \qquad \text{(A.3.4)}$$

The solution to the homogenous part of (A.3.4) is:

$$k(t) = b_2 e^{(A - \delta - n)t}, \qquad \text{(A.3.5)}$$

while the solution to the non-homogenous part, $\tilde{k}(t)$, can be found as follows (e.g. Gandolfo, 1996, pp. 161/162):

$$\tilde{k}(t) = -e^{(A - \delta - n)t} \int \left[\bar{c} + b_1 e^{\theta^{-1}(A - \delta - \rho)t} \right] e^{-(A - \delta - n)t} dt, \qquad \text{(A.3.6)}$$

and integration finally yields,

$$\tilde{k}(t) = \frac{\bar{c}}{A - \delta - n} - \frac{b_1 e^{\theta^{-1}(A - \delta - \rho)t}}{\theta^{-1}(A - \delta - \rho) - (A - \delta - n)} - \alpha e^{(A - \delta - n)t} \qquad \text{(A.3.7)}$$

where α denotes an arbitrary constant of integration. Finally, the general solution of the non-homogenous differential equation (A.3.4) is as follows:

$$k(t) = (b_2 - \alpha)e^{(A - \delta - n)t} + \frac{\bar{c}}{A - \delta - n} - \frac{b_1 e^{\theta^{-1}(A - \delta - \rho)t}}{\theta^{-1}(A - \delta - \rho) - (A - \delta - n)}. \qquad \text{(A.3.8)}$$

By noting the dynamic efficiency condition (3.7) the transversality condition, stated in footnote 61, can be expressed in the following form:

$$\lim_{t \to \infty} \left[\lambda(0)e^{-(A - \delta - n)t} k(t) \right] = 0, \qquad \text{(A.3.9)}$$

and inserting (A.3.8) into the transversality condition gives:

$$\lim_{t\to\infty}\lambda(0)\left[b_2-\alpha+\frac{\bar{c}e^{-(A-\delta-n)\cdot t}}{A-\delta-n}+\frac{b_1e^{-[A-\delta-n-\theta^{-1}(A-\delta-\rho)]\cdot t}}{A-\delta-n-\theta^{-1}(A-\delta-\rho)}\right]=0. \quad (A.3.10)$$

The finiteness of the utility integral in (3.3) requires $A-\delta-n-\theta^{-1}(A-\delta-\rho)>0$ (Barro and Sala-i-Martin, 1995, pp. 142/143). Consequently, the third term inside the brackets in (A.3.10) vanishes asymptotically. The second term vanishes asymptotically as well provided that $A-\delta-n>0$. This parameter restriction inevitably follows in the case of growth, i.e. $A-\delta-\rho>0$. In the case of regress, $A-\delta-\rho<0$, it represents an additional restriction (which does not contradict any other parameter restriction). Consequently, the transversality condition requires $b_2-\alpha$ to equal zero and the optimal solutions read as follows:

$$c(t)=\bar{c}+b_1e^{\theta^{-1}(A-\delta-\rho)\cdot t} \quad (A.3.11)$$

$$k(t)=\frac{\bar{c}}{A-\delta-n}+\frac{b_1e^{\theta^{-1}(A-\delta-\rho)\cdot t}}{A-\delta-n-\theta^{-1}(A-\delta-\rho)}. \quad (A.3.12)$$

From (A.3.12) it follows that the constant b_1 is determined by:

$$b_1=z[k(0)-\bar{k}]$$

with

$$\bar{k}\equiv\frac{\bar{c}}{A-\delta-n}\quad\text{and}\quad z\equiv A-\delta-n-\theta^{-1}(A-\delta-\rho). \quad (A.3.13)$$

According to (3.3) the initial value of capital per capita is predetermined. The corresponding value of the control variable can be easily determined by using the policy function, which immediately results from (A.3.11) and (A.3.12):

$$c(0)=z[k(0)-\bar{k}]+\bar{c} \quad (A.3.14)$$

For each value of $k(0)$ there is a unique optimal choice of $c(0)$ which satisfies all first-order conditions, including the transversality condition. This is the contents of the policy function (A.3.14).

Appendix 3-2: The rate of convergence

The analytical expressions for the instantaneous rate of convergence according to the definition (3.18) based on both the c/k-ratio and the logarithm of the c/k-ratio are as follows:

$$\lambda[c(t)/k(t)] = -\frac{\dfrac{\left(\bar{k}+\dfrac{b_1}{z}e^{w \cdot t}\right)wb_1 e^{w \cdot t}-\left(\bar{c}+b_1 e^{w \cdot t}\right)\dfrac{wb_1}{z}e^{w \cdot t}}{\left(\bar{k}+\dfrac{b_1}{z}e^{w \cdot t}\right)^2}}{\dfrac{\bar{c}+b_1 e^{w \cdot t}}{\bar{k}+\dfrac{b_1}{z}e^{w \cdot t}}-z}$$

(A.3.15)

$$\lambda[\ln(c(t)/k(t))] = -\frac{\dfrac{\left(\bar{k}+\dfrac{b_1}{z}e^{w \cdot t}\right)wb_1 e^{w \cdot t}-\left(\bar{c}+b_1 e^{w \cdot t}\right)\dfrac{wb_1}{z}e^{w \cdot t}}{\left(\bar{k}+\dfrac{b_1}{z}e^{w \cdot t}\right)\cdot\left(\bar{c}+b_1 e^{w \cdot t}\right)}}{\ln\left(\dfrac{\bar{c}+b_1 e^{w \cdot t}}{\bar{k}+\dfrac{b_1}{z}e^{w \cdot t}}\right)-\ln(z)}$$

(A.3.16)

With $\bar{k} \equiv \dfrac{\bar{c}}{A-\delta-n}$, $w \equiv \theta^{-1}(A-\delta-\rho)$, and
$z \equiv A-\delta-n-\theta^{-1}(A-\delta-\rho)$.

The preceding expressions show that the instantaneous rate of convergence depends on time, technology and preference parameters, as well as initial conditions expressed in b_1.

Appendix 3-3: Sets of parameters

Table 3.2. Sets of parameters

King and Rebelo (1993, p. 916); RCK model with technical progress.	$\theta = 1$ and $\theta = 10$, $\delta = 0.1$, $n = 0.014$, ($\alpha = 0.33$, $\alpha = 0.5$, and $\alpha = 0.9$)
Easterly (1994, p. 534); JM model with SG preferences	$\theta = 1$, $\delta = 0.05$, $\rho = 0.1$, $n = 0.02$ ($\tau = 0.2$)

Table 3.2. continued

Sarel (1994, p. 4); RCK model with technical progress	$\theta = 1.5$, $\delta = 0.04$, $\rho = 0.02$, $n = 0$ ($x = 0.01$ and $\alpha = 0.4$)
Barro and Sala-i-Martin (1995, p. 83); RCK model with technical progress	$\theta = 3$, $\delta = 0.05$, $\rho = 0.02$, $n = 0.01$, ($x = 0.02$, $\alpha = 0.3$ and $\alpha = 0.75$)
Maußner and Klump (1996, p. 128); RCK model without technical progress	$\theta = 3$, $\delta + n = 0.05$, $\rho = 0.01$, ($\alpha = 0.33$ and $\alpha = 0.66$)
Ortigueira and Santos (1997, p. 390); RCK model without technical progress	$\theta = 1.5$, $\delta = 0.05$, $\rho = 0.05$, $n = 0.01$ ($x = 0.01$ and $\alpha = 0.4$)
Barro (1990, p. S110); linear growth model with two types of capital (private and public).	$\theta = 1$, $\delta = 0$, $\rho = 0.02$, $n = 0$, ($\alpha = 0.25$)

JM: Jones-Manuelli, RCK: Ramsey-Cass-Koopmans, SG: Stone-Geary. α denotes the capital share, δ the depreciation rate of capital, θ the elasticity of marginal utility, n the growth rate of population, x the rate of (exogenous) technical progress, and ρ the time preference rate, respectively.

3.6.2 The Jones-Manuelli model with subsistence consumption

Appendix 3-4: Stability of stationary dynamic equilibria

Linearising the differential equation system (3.26) and (3.27) by means of a Taylor approximation of first order around any stationary point ($\hat{c},\hat{k}$) gives:

$$\dot{c} \cong \theta^{-1}\left[(1-\tau)\cdot\left(A+\alpha B\hat{k}^{\alpha-1}\right)-\delta-\rho\right]\cdot(c-\hat{c})$$
$$+(\hat{c}-\overline{c})\theta^{-1}(1-\tau)\alpha(\alpha-1)B\hat{k}^{\alpha-2}\cdot\left(k-\hat{k}\right) \tag{A.3.17}$$

$$\dot{k} \cong -(c-\hat{c})+\left[(1-\tau)\cdot\left(A+\alpha B\hat{k}^{\alpha-1}\right)-\delta-n\right]\cdot\left(k-\hat{k}\right) \tag{A.3.18}$$

The Jacobian matrix accordingly reads:

$$\mathbf{J}=\begin{pmatrix} \theta^{-1}\left[(1-\tau)\cdot\left(A+\alpha B\hat{k}^{\alpha-1}\right)-\delta-\rho\right] & (\hat{c}-\overline{c})\theta^{-1}(1-\tau)\alpha(\alpha-1)B\hat{k}^{\alpha-2} \\ -1 & (1-\tau)\cdot\left(A+\alpha B\hat{k}^{\alpha-1}\right)-\delta-n \end{pmatrix}.$$
$$\tag{A.3.19}$$

and the Jacobian determinant is

$$|\mathbf{J}| = \theta^{-1}\left[(1-\tau)\cdot\left(A+\alpha B\hat{k}^{\alpha-1}\right)-\delta-\rho\right]\cdot\left[(1-\tau)\cdot\left(A+\alpha B\hat{k}^{\alpha-1}\right)-(\delta+n)\right]$$
$$+\left(\hat{c}-\overline{c}\right)\theta^{-1}(1-\tau)\alpha(\alpha-1)B\hat{k}^{\alpha-2}.$$

(A.3.20)

In order to prove for local stability properties of the differential equation system (3.26) and (3.27), the determinant of the Jacobian has to be evaluated at the two stationary points: $(\overline{c},\overline{k})$, (c^*,k^*), where $\overline{c}$ is a constant positive parameter, $\overline{k}$ is a positive constant too, defined implicitly by $(1-\tau)\cdot\left(A\overline{k}+B\overline{k}^{\alpha}\right)-(\delta+n)\overline{k}-\overline{c}=0$, [96] $c^*=\left[(1-\tau)A-(\delta+n)\right]k^*+B(k^*)^{\alpha}$,

and $k^* = \left(\dfrac{\delta+\rho-(1-\tau)A}{(1-\tau)\alpha B}\right)^{\frac{1}{\alpha-1}}$.

The subsistence equilibrium $(\overline{c},\overline{k})$ requires $(1-\tau)\cdot\left(A+\alpha B\overline{k}^{\alpha-1}\right)-\delta-\rho<0$. In addition, the last term in (A.3.20) equals zero for $\hat{c}=\overline{c}$. Hence, the subsistence equilibrium is saddle-point stable, i.e. $|\mathbf{J}|<0$, provided that $(1-\tau)\cdot\left(A+\alpha B\overline{k}^{\alpha-1}\right)-(\delta+n)>0$.[97] This requirement seems not to be very restrictive since the production function satisfies one of the Inada conditions: $\lim_{k\to 0}\partial y/\partial k=\infty$.

The steady state with consumption above subsistence (c^*,k^*), requires $(1-\tau)\cdot\left[A+\alpha B(k^*)^{\alpha-1}\right]-\delta-\rho=0$ and therefore the Jacobian determinant reads: $|\mathbf{J}|=\left(c^*-\overline{c}\right)\theta^{-1}(1-\tau)\alpha(\alpha-1)B(k^*)^{\alpha-2}$. The Jacobian determinant is negative because $0<\alpha<1$ and hence (c^*,k^*) is (locally) saddle-point stable either.

Appendix 3-5: Stability of the asymptotic balanced-growth equilibrium

The proof of (local) stability properties of the asymptotic balanced-growth equilibrium comprises two steps (Koch, 1999): (i) The asymptotic direction of the BGP^{∞} is determined and (ii) the asymptotic eigenvalues of the

[96] As has been noted already, this equation might have two solutions for $\overline{k}$; one less than the golden-rule value for k and one greater. In this case, the lower value is the relevant one (Easterly, 1994, p. 531).
[97] Because the determinant of the Jacobian equals the product of its eigenvalues, a negative determinant means that the eigenvalues (or characteristic roots) are of opposite signs. This immediately implies saddle-point stability in the case of stationary equilibria (e.g. Chiang, 1984, pp. 641-643 and Lorenz, 1989, pp. 16-21).

Jacobian of the differential equation system along this direction are calculated.

In order to determine the asymptotic direction of the BGP^{∞}, it is as-
sumed that $c = Dk$ for some unknown D, i.e. $\lim\limits_{k \to \infty} \dfrac{\dot{c}(k,Dk)}{\dot{k}(k,Dk)} = D$ has to be
solved for D:

$$\lim_{k \to \infty} \frac{Dk\theta^{-1}\left[(1-\tau)(A+\alpha Bk^{\alpha-1})-\delta-\rho\right]-\bar{c}\theta^{-t}\left[(1-\tau)(A+\alpha Bk^{\alpha-1})-\delta-\rho\right]}{(1-\tau)(Ak+Bk^{\alpha})-(\delta+n)k-Dk}$$

$$= D.$$

(A.3.21)

Applying L'Hôpital's rule, one gets:

$$\lim_{k \to \infty} \frac{D\theta^{-1}\left[(1-\tau)\cdot(A+\alpha^2 Bk^{\alpha-1})-\delta-\rho)\right]-\bar{c}\theta^{-1}(1-\tau)\alpha(\alpha-1)Bk^{\alpha-2}}{(1-\tau)\cdot(A+\alpha Bk^{\alpha-1})-\delta-n-D} = D.$$

(A.3.22)

Noting that $0 < \alpha < 1$ the preceding equation reduces to:

$$\frac{D\theta^{-1}\left[(1-\tau)A-\delta-\rho\right]}{(1-\tau)A-\delta-n-D} = D,$$

(A.3.23)

which has two solutions $D_1 = 0$ and
$D_2 = (1-\tau)A-\delta-n-\theta^{-1}\left[(1-\tau)A-\delta-\rho\right]$. The trajectory associated with
the asymptotic direction $D_1 = 0$ violates the transversality condition stated
in footnote 83 and hence has to be excluded.[98] The latter solution shows the
(asymptotic) direction of the BGP^{∞} which equals the 6direction of the
BGP of the linear growth model (e.g. Barro and Sala-i-Martin, 1995, p.
143).

In the next step, the Jacobian matrix of the underlying differential
equation system is calculated and the limit of its eigenvalues is taken for
$c = Dk$ and $k \to \infty$. The Jacobian of (3.26) and (3.27) reads:

---

[98] The dynamic efficiency condition (3.23) indicates that the asymptotic growth rate of the
term $e^{-(\rho-n)\cdot t}\lambda(t)$ is $\delta+n-(1-\tau)A$. With respect to (3.27) the asymptotic growth
rate of k in the case of $\gamma_c < \gamma_k$ is $(1-\tau)A-\delta-n$. Hence, the transversality condition would be violated (e.g. Barro and Sala-i-Martin, 1995, p. 65).

$$\mathbf{J} = \begin{pmatrix} \theta^{-1}\left[(1-\tau)\cdot\left(A+\alpha Bk^{\alpha-1}\right)-\delta-\rho\right] & (c-\bar{c})\theta^{-1}(1-\tau)\alpha(\alpha-1)Bk^{\alpha-2} \\ -1 & (1-\tau)\cdot\left(A+\alpha Bk^{\alpha-1}\right)-\delta-n \end{pmatrix}.$$

$$(\text{A.3.24})$$

The eigenvalues (or characteristic roots) of $\mathbf{J}$ are the solutions to $\left|\mathbf{J}-\lambda\mathbf{I}\right|=0$, which gives:

$$\left\{\theta^{-1}\left[(1-\tau)\cdot\left(A+\alpha Bk^{\alpha-1}\right)-\delta-\rho\right]-\lambda\right\}\cdot\left\{(1-\tau)\cdot\left(A+\alpha Bk^{\alpha-1}\right)-\delta-n-\lambda\right\}$$
$$+(c-\bar{c})\theta^{-1}\left[(1-\tau)\alpha(\alpha-1)Bk^{\alpha-2}\right]=0$$

$$(\text{A.3.25})$$

The limit of the eigenvalues for $c=Dk$ and $k\to\infty$ are the solution to:

$$\left\{\theta^{-1}\left[(1-\tau)A-\delta-\rho\right]-\lambda\right\}\cdot\left\{(1-\tau)A-\delta-n-\lambda\right\}=0, \qquad (\text{A.3.26})$$

which implies that $\lambda_1=\theta^{-1}\left[(1-\tau)A-\delta-\rho\right]$ and $\lambda_2=(1-\tau)A-\delta-n$. Both eigenvalues are positive.[99] λ_1 is the asymptotic balanced growth rate. Hence $\lambda_2>0$ implies that the BGP^∞ with the asymptotic slope $D>0$ is saddle-point stable and all other trajectory diverge, i.e. the optimal solution is unique (Koch, 1999, Theorem 3.1).[100]

---

[99] Unbounded growth requires $\theta^{-1}\left[(1-\tau)A-\delta-\rho\right]>0$. The finiteness of the utility integral requires that $(1-\tau)A-\delta-n-\theta^{-1}\left[(1-\tau)A-\delta-\rho\right]>0$ (e.g. Barro and Sala-i-Martin, 1995, pp. 142/143) and hence $(1-\tau)A-\delta-n>0$.

[100] The saddle point can be labelled 'infinite horizon saddle point' because the model in question shows unbounded growth (Koch, 1999, p. 9).

4 Productive consumption and growth in developing countries

4.1 Introduction

The common interest of nearly all development and growth theories is the fundamental concept of the 'harsh' intertemporal consumption trade-off: Current consumption inevitably reduces future consumption possibilities in a with-or-without sense. This is true for the early 'low-level-equilibrium-trap theories' (Nelson, 1956 and Leibenstein, 1957), the neoclassical growth theory (Solow, 1956; Swan, 1956; Ramsey, 1928; Cass, 1965; and Koopmans, 1965) as well as the for endogenous growth theories (e.g. Lucas, 1988; Romer, 1990; and Rebelo, 1991).

In contrast, already since the fifties the possibility of productive consumption was recognised within the development literature (Winslow, 1951 and Nurkse, 1953).[101] *Productive consumption* enables the satisfaction of current needs and, at the same time, increases the productive potential of labour.[102] As a consequence, the potential for the satisfaction of future needs rises. Two basic interpretations of the productive effect of consumption can be distinguished: First, productive consumption can be interpreted as enhancing the stock of human capital (Blaug, 1987). Second, productive consumption can be considered as increasing the efficiency of labour. This second interpretation underlies the traditional efficiency wage theory (Leibenstein, 1957; Stiglitz, 1976; and Bliss and Stern, 1978).

Gersovitz (1988, pp. 394-396) distinguishes three forms of productive consumption: (i) nutrition; (ii) health efforts; and (iii) education.[103] All three forms serve the satisfaction of current needs and hence can be labelled as consumption expenditures; though occasionally this might be assessed differently in the case of education. At the same time, the stock of

---

[101] Compare further, Wheeler (1980) and Gersovitz (1983). The basic idea of productive consumption has already been recognised and discussed by classical economists in the context of the subsistence theory of wages (Blaug, 1987).

[102] The question whether specific investment expenditures are registered as investment or consumption expenditures within the framework of national accounting is irrelevant for the purpose of theoretical analysis.

[103] However, Gersovitz (1988) does not use the term 'productive consumption'.

human capital enhances or – depending on the interpretation – the efficiency of labour increases. From this point of view, the underlying consumption activities can be classified as productive. Gersovitz (1988, p. 396) expresses this notion as follows: *"Health and nutrition expenditures share some attributes of educational ones; they affect welfare beyond the period when they are made. To a much greater extent than in the case of education, however, these expenditures also affect current well-being, and it would be impossible to devise a convincing allocation of these expenditures between current and future consumption. For instance, at low nutritional levels, food consumption has joint effects on current and future wellbeing and productivity."*

For developing countries (DCs) special characteristics of preferences and technology exist, which are relevant to growth. For example, intertemporal preferences are usually assumed to exhibit a constant time preference rate though a negative relation between the time preference rate and per capita income seems reasonable, especially for the lower range of income.[104] With respect to technology, the effect of enhancing the stock of human capital or increasing the efficiency of labour as a consequence of consumption activities represents a further characteristic relevant to growth, which has been almost completely ignored in the context of growth theory.[105] After reviewing empirical evidence in favour of a positive nutrition-productivity relation, Fogel (1994, pp. 385/386) states: *"Although largely neglected by theorists of both the 'old' and the 'new' growth economics, these factors can easily be incorporated into standard growth models."* The growth models discussed in Sections 4.3.1 and 4.3.2 represent an attempt to incorporate the productive-consumption hypothesis into simple endogenous growth models.

From the perspective of growth theory, the productive-consumption hypothesis seems to be of fundamental interest because of two reasons: First, productive consumption essentially modifies, i.e. partially eliminates, the intertemporal consumption trade-off.[106] Second, theoretical and empirical

---

[104] This relation is known as the Fisher-hypothesis (Fisher, 1907). Usually, if the time preference rate is allowed to be endogenous, a positive relation between the time preference rate and per capita income is postulated, mainly because of technical reasons in order to guarantee stability. For a discussion on this subject see Obstfeld (1990) as well as Zee (1994).

[105] To the best of my knowledge, the only exception is Wichmann (1996), who formulates a two-sector growth model with the labour efficiency being dependent on nutrition. However, Wichman interprets the nutrition-productivity relation as an external effect which is not relevant for the individual choice of an optimal consumption path. Therefore, this model does not capture the crucial point considered in this chapter, which is the modification of the harsh intertemporal consumption trade-off.

[106] That is, as far as the possibility of productive consumption exists. The hypothesis of productive consumption does not assert that every consumption activity is productive.

evidence suggests a systematic negative relation between the level of consumption per capita and the marginal productive effect of consumption.[107] To concentrate on the importance of productive consumption for economic growth does surely not intend to neglect the importance of other factors that undoubtedly influence growth and development, e.g. the stability of the political system, the openness of the economy, or the development of the financial sector.

This chapter is organised as follows: In Section 4.2 first of all a brief outline of the current theoretical and empirical work on the subject 'productive consumption' is given. The implications of the productive-consumption hypothesis for the intertemporal consumption trade-off as well as its implications for the process of growth are investigated in Section 4.3. The analysis follows the basic interpretations of the productive-consumption hypothesis as explained above. Accordingly, in Section 4.3.1 the productive-consumption effect is interpreted as enhancing the stock of human capital while in Section 4.3.2 the productive-consumption effect is considered as increasing the efficiency of labour.

4.2 Productive consumption: an overview

4.2.1 Empirical evidence

The relation between labour productivity and output growth on the one hand and nutrition, health efforts, and education on the other hand has been analysed empirically mainly against the background of two different questions: (i) In the wake of the traditional efficiency wage theory, it has been attempted to uncover empirical evidence supporting or refuting the impact of nutrition and health expenditures on labour productivity within the framework of microeconomic empirical analyses.[108] (ii) On the other hand, the contribution of nutrition, health efforts, and education to output growth has been examined on a macroeconomic level using the methods of growth accounting. These empirical investigations were partly motivated by the question whether a development strategy primarily focusing on the satisfaction of basic needs prevents an economy from growing or even stimulates growth (Hicks, 1979; Wheeler, 1980; and Barro and Sala-i-Martin, 1995, Chapter 12). Some selected empirical investigations and their most important results are outlined subsequently.

---

[107] For empirical evidence see Section 4.2.1. Within the framework of the efficiency wage theory, this assumption is represented by the so-called effort-function (see Section 4.2.2).

[108] Behrman and Deolalikar (1988) outline the empirical investigations concerning the efficiency wage theory.

Microeconomic analyses

On the basis of microeconomic cross-sectional data for small-scale farming enterprises in Sierra Leone (1974/75), Strauss (1986) estimates the coefficients of an agricultural Cobb-Douglas production function. The production function is specified to account for a dependence of the workers' efficiency upon daily nutrient intake per worker. The approach takes into account the simultaneity between the choices of the households and the levels of variable farm inputs and it considers the possible influence of other variables on agricultural output like land quality for example. The coefficients of nutrient intake show the expected positive sign and are highly significant. The positive impact of nutrient intake on labour productivity is especially marked at low levels and decreases with an increasing level of calorie intake. The estimation results imply remarkably high values for the elasticity of output with respect to nutrition at low levels of calorie intake. The corresponding values vary from 0.49 at a daily intake of 1500 calories via 0.34 at the sample mean value for a daily calorie intake up to 0.12 at a daily intake of 4500 calories (Strauss, 1986, pp. 313/314).[109] Accordingly, at the mean value of daily calorie intake, an increase by 1 per cent results in a rise in output by 0.34 per cent.

Deolalikar (1988) investigates, based upon Strauss (1986), the relation between labour productivity in agriculture as well as the wage rate of rural workers on the one hand and individual calorie intake per day and weight-for-height (kg per cm) on the other hand by using panel data for 240 households in different rural areas of southern India (1976-77 and 1977-78). In this case, the weight-for-height variable is interpreted as a medium-term indicator of the nutritional status and as an indicator of the health status. The results are ambiguous: The coefficients of calorie intake per day are not significant, while the coefficients of weight-for-height prove to be significant. However, Deolalikar (1988, p. 412) does not interpret these results as an evidence against a nutrition-productivity relation: *"What the empirical results then suggest is that, even if the short-run effects of nutrition on labor productivity are insignificant, the medium-run effects are large and positive. [...] Another interpretation may simply be that weight-for-height is a better indicator than average daily calorie intake."*

In the context of a mesoeconomic study, Ram and Schultz (1979) analyse the relation between health status and labour productivity in agriculture based on data for different Indian states. The rate of mortality is employed as an indicator of the health status. Accordingly, a decrease in the rate of mortality is interpreted as an improvement in the health status. The authors regress the percentage change in rural labour productivity on the

---

[109] Wolgenmuth *et al.* (1982) find similarly high values for output elasticity with respect to calorie intake for Kenyan road construction workers.

percentage change in the rate of mortality for the period from 1958-67. This univariate regression explains 28 per cent of the interstate variation in agricultural productivity; the corresponding coefficient amounts to 0.3 and is highly significant. Consequently, a reduction in the rate of mortality by 1 percentage point increases the labour productivity by 0.3 percentage points.

Macroeconomic analyses

On a macroeconomic level, Wheeler (1980) examines the relation between the growth rate of output on the one hand and the growth rate of different indicators of the nutritional status (calorie availability per day), the health status (life expectancy at birth), and education (adult literacy rate), on the other hand, for 54 DCs (1960-70). For this purpose, Wheeler formulates a simultaneous four-equation model, consisting of a macroeconomic production function and one equation for nutrition, health, and education, respectively (which are called 'welfare equations').[110] The production function includes capital in addition to labour in efficiency units as inputs, with the latter again depending on the level of nutrition, health, and education.[111] The three 'welfare equations' represent the level of nutrition, health, and education as a function of per capita income as well as some exogenous variables. By this formulation, a mutual causality between the growth rate of output on the one hand and the change in nutrition, health, and education on the other hand can be taken into consideration. Wheeler finds a strong labour augmenting effect of the nutrition and health variables in the determination of the change in output for 'poor countries'. The parameter estimates imply an elasticity of effective labour with respect to nutrition of 11.14 and an elasticity of effective labour with respect to health of 7.13. Multiplying these elasticities with the elasticity of output with respect to effective labour yields the elasticity of output with respect to nutrition ($0.26 \cdot 11.14 \cong 2.90$) and the elasticity of output with respect to health ($0.26 \cdot 7.13 \cong 1.85$). These values are several times higher compared to the microeconomic elasticities of Strauss (1986). A possible interpretation is based on the assumption of positive external effects of the effi-

---

[110] This model is purely econometric in order to derive estimation equations for the growth rate of output while explicitly taking into account simultaneity. The model is not able to achieve a theoretical analysis of the importance of the productive effects of nutrition, health, and education for the growth process.

[111] Consequently, the production function in Cobb-Douglas form reads:

$Q_t = A_t K_t^{\gamma_1} (L_t H_t^{\theta_1} N_t^{\theta_2} E_t^{\theta_3})^{\gamma_2}$, where Q_t denotes output, A_t the level of technology, K_t the capital stock, L_t physical labour, H_t a health indicator, N_t a nutritional indicator, and E_t an indicator of the educational level at time t, respectively.

ciency of labour: Well nourished, healthy, appropriately educated, and economically active individuals increase the productivity of other economically active individuals.[112] Somewhat surprisingly, Wheeler finds no significant influence of education on the growth rate of output; not even at the 10 per cent level of significance. Furthermore, the analysis of the productive contributions of nutrition, health efforts, and education reveals a strong influence of nutrition and health efforts especially for low per capita incomes and a decreasing marginal contribution with a rise in per capita income, while the positive influence of education increases with a rise in per capita income. Wheeler (1980, p. 450) summarises his econometric analysis with the words: *"Thus, the available data are shown to be consistent with the notion that some basic needs expenditures can legitimately be regarded as investments in human capital."*

The above-mentioned results are confirmed by Hicks (1979). He finds, without exception, a strong and significant influence of different 'basic-needs' indicators (life expectancy at birth, adult literacy rate, primary school enrolment rates) on the growth rate of real per capita income within the framework of different multiple regressions based on cross-sectional data for 69 non-oilexporting DCs (1960-73). Barro (1991) finds a positive and highly significant influence of life expectancy at birth, interpreted as a nutrition and health indicator, on the growth rate of real per capita income within the framework of a broadly designed cross-sectional analysis; whereas the results for various indicators of education are ambiguous.[113] Finally, Fogel (1994) estimates the importance of a nutrition-productivity relation for the development process of Britain. He concludes that improvements in nutrition explain 30 per cent of per capita income growth between 1790 and 1980. One third of this effect is assigned to increased labour force participation while the remaining two thirds are assigned to an increased labour productivity.

4.2.2 Theoretical approaches

4.2.2.1 Preliminary remarks

Traditional efficiency wage theory supposes a positive relation between the level of consumption and the efficiency of labour. This hypothesis bears far-reaching theoretical implications with respect to the labour market: Profit-maximising producers offer that wage rate which minimises the cost

---

[112] See Lucas (1988), who assumes positive external effects of the average human capital stock in the production of output. However, a direct comparison between the results of Strauss (1986) and the results of Wheeler (1980) is problematic on account of different references to space and time.

[113] In addition, see Barro and Sala-i-Martin (1995, Chapter 12).

of labour in units of efficiency; this wage is called the efficiency wage. If the market-clearing wage rate lies below the efficiency wage unemployment arises. The traditional efficiency wage theory primarily explains the widespread phenomenon of rural unemployment in DCs (Stiglitz, 1976 and Bliss and Stern, 1978).[114]

The implications of a positive relation between consumption and the efficiency of labour – in other words the implications of the productive-consumption hypothesis – for the consumption/ saving behaviour were hardly analysed within economic literature.[115] Gersovitz (1983) represents an important exception. He discusses two complementary approaches, which analyse explicitly the importance of productive consumption for the consumption/ saving behaviour within the framework of discrete two-period models.[116] Both approaches are based on the idea that consumption might have a second positive effect in addition to the direct satisfaction of current needs. This additional effect consists in an increase in the probability of survival and in an increase in the efficiency of labour. Both approaches imply a positive relation between the average saving rate and income based on sound microeconomic foundations.[117] Both approaches are outlined in their essential features because of their exceptional importance for theoretical analysis.

4.2.2.2   Consumption and the probability of survival

The crucial hypothesis of the first model is a positive relation between the standard of living and the probability of survival for the lower range of income. Consequently, consumption increases welfare in two different respects: The satisfaction of current needs means a (traditional) direct utility effect. The indirect utility effect of consumption consists in an increase in the probability of survival. The importance of this additional consumption effect decreases with an increase in the standard of living.

The individual considered exists for two periods (presence and future) and solely receives income in the first period. This income, y, is divided

---

[114] During the eighties, the efficiency wage theory has been further developed within the framework of new-keynesian theory and used to explain real wage rigidities and unemployment in industrialised economies (Yellen, 1984 and Romer, 1996, Chapter 10).

[115] Empirical investigations of the saving behaviour in DCs usually test the validity of the absolute-income-, the permanent-income- and the life-cycle hypothesis (e.g. Mikesell and Zinser, 1973). For more current investigations see Aghevli et al. (1990) and Reichel (1993).

[116] However, Gersovitz (1983) does not use the term 'productive consumption', instead he discusses the "...physiological consequences of poor nutrition associated with low income." Gersovitz (1983, p. 842).

[117] A positive relation between the saving rate and income already results from the keynesian absolute-income hypothesis which is based on the behavioural assumptions of an autonomous consumption and a constant marginal rate of consumption.

up between current consumption, c_1, and savings, s. Future consumption, c_2, equals current savings multiplied by an interest rate factor, R:

$$y = c + s \tag{4.1}$$

$$c_2 = Rs. \tag{4.2}$$

The probability of surviving the first period, π, increases with the level of consumption during the first period. Furthermore, a concave and twice continuously differentiable 'survival-probability function' is assumed:

$$\pi = \pi(c_1) \quad \text{with} \quad \pi' > 0 \quad \text{and} \quad \pi'' \leq 0.\text{[118]} \tag{4.3}$$

The individual chooses c_1 and c_2 in order to maximise the expected lifetime utility, Eu,

$$Eu = u(c_1) + \pi(c_1)u(c_2), \tag{4.4}$$

with respect to (4.1) and (4.2).[119] The instantaneous utility function, $u(c)$, is also assumed to be concave and twice continuously differentiable. Application of the Lagrangian method yields the first-order condition for an interior solution, i.e. $c_1, c_2 > 0$:

$$u'(c_1) + \pi'(c_1)u(c_2) = R\pi(c_1)u'(c_2). \tag{4.5}$$

An optimal solution requires that the marginal gain in welfare due to an increase in current consumption equals the marginal gain in welfare due to an increase in future consumption.[120] The left-hand side of (4.5) shows the marginal increase in welfare resulting from current consumption, which consists of two components. A marginal increase in current consumption causes the expected lifetime utility to rise according to the marginal utility of current consumption, $u'(c_1)$, and, additionally, according to a rise in the expected future utility, resulting from an increase in the probability of survival, $\pi'(c_1) \cdot u(c_2)$. The right-hand side of (4.5) shows the marginal increase in welfare due to an increase in future consumption. The probability of experiencing the future is, of course, considered for the calculation of the expected value.

---

[118] Gersovitz (1983, p. 844) justifies the shape of this function merely on account of the plausibility of this assumption.

[119] Discounting future utility by means of a time preference rate is not considered in (4.4). Future utility is nonetheless 'discounted' by means of the probability of survival which is assumed to be smaller than unity.

[120] A sufficient condition for a maximum is a concave 'survival-probability-function'; the validity of this assumption is presupposed by Gersovitz (1983).

Gersovitz discusses two threshold effects: Below a subsistence level of consumption, $\tilde{c}$, survival is impossible, i.e. $\pi(c_1 < \tilde{c}) = 0$. If income falls short of this subsistence level, saving is zero, $c_2 = s = 0$. A second threshold effect appears as soon as the initial level of consumption exceeds a value above which no further influence on the probability of survival exists, $\pi(c_1 > \hat{c}_1) = \bar{\pi}$. Without this 'survival effect' of consumption, $\pi \equiv 1$, condition (4.5) turns into the usual optimum condition:

$$u'(c_1) = Ru'(c_2).\tag{4.6}$$

As long as the utility function is isoelastic and the interest rate equals zero, a positive relation between the average saving rate and income exists, provided that:

$$\gamma + \lambda(\eta - 1) > 0 \quad \text{where} \quad \lambda \equiv \frac{c_2}{c_1} \qquad \eta \equiv -\frac{\pi''c_1}{\pi'}\tag{4.7}$$

and γ denotes the elasticity of utility with respect to consumption. Condition (4.7) is fulfilled whenever the elasticity of the marginal probability of survival with respect to consumption, η, is greater than unity. Provided that the marginal probability of survival declines sufficiently fast in response to current consumption, the individual is willing to increase future consumption more than proportionately as income rises, thereby increasing the saving rate.[121]

4.2.2.3 Consumption and the productivity of labour

As mentioned above, traditional efficiency wage theory assumes a positive impact of the individual wage rate on the efficiency of labour. In this context, a higher wage rate is implicitly assumed to induce an increase in the level of consumption. Due to a 'physiological-technological' relation a higher productivity per man-hour results. By means of a second model, Gersovitz (1983) analyses the resulting implications for the individual saving behaviour. He describes the productive consumption effect and its possible implication for the saving behaviour as follows: "*Greater current consumption adds to utility directly and indirectly by increasing income, thereby creating a bias against saving.*" Gersovitz (1983, p. 848).

The crucial hypothesis of consumption, c_1, enhancing the efficiency of labour, h, is represented by a mixed convex-concave and twice continuously differentiable 'effort-function'. In accordance with the efficiency

---

[121] For further interpretations see Gersovitz (1983, p. 845).

wage literature it is supposed that consumption increases the efficiency of labour without any delay: [122]

$$h = h(c_1) \qquad \text{with} \qquad h' \geq 0. \tag{4.8}$$

The individual considered exists for two periods, the entire income is received exclusively during the first period and experience of the second period is – in contrast to the former model – certain. Current and future consumption are chosen in order to maximise total utility,

$$V = u(c_1) + u(c_2), \tag{4.9}$$

subject to the constraints,

$$Rs = c_2 \tag{4.10}$$

$$c_1 + s = y = wh(c_1) + \alpha. \tag{4.11}$$

In this case w denotes the wage rate per efficiency unit of labour, i.e. the wage rate per man-hour in relation to one unit of efficient labour, $h(c_1)$ the efficiency of labour, so that $wh(c_1)$ represents wage income and α all non-wage income. The first-order condition for an interior solution reads:

$$u'(c_1) = -Ru'(c_2) \cdot (wh' - 1). \tag{4.12}$$

Taking into consideration the presumed positive marginal utility, condition (4.12) can only be fulfilled if the following inequality holds:

$$(wh' - 1) < 0 \qquad \text{or} \qquad wh' < 1. \tag{4.13}$$

The interpretation of condition (4.13) is as follows: Saving necessarily means a reduction in current consumption. Consequently, the efficiency of labour and wage income decreases in accordance with the effort-function. The condition $wh' < 1$ means that further saving, i.e. renunciation of current consumption, by one unit can only be reasonable if the induced reduction in income turns out to be smaller. The bias towards current consumption for low incomes can be seen more clearly if (4.12) is reworded to:

$$u'(c_1) = Ru'(c_2) - Ru'(c_2)wh'. \tag{4.12a}$$

For low incomes and low levels of consumption, h' is comparably high, and the value of the right-hand side of (4.12a) is comparably small. Hence, a low marginal utility of consumption in the first period (left-hand side) and, taking into account the concavity of the utility function, a com-

---

[122] Gersovitz employs an effort-function, $h(c)$, which possesses a mixed convex-concave shape. Within the efficiency-wage literature, convex-concave effort-functions as well as globally concave effort-functions have been employed (Rosenzweig, 1988, pp. 720).

parably high level of current consumption results. This effect disappears with a rise in income and for $h' = 0$ (4.12a) turns into the usual optimum condition.

The average saving rate rises with income provided that the following condition holds:[123]

$$(1 + \lambda) \cdot (\varepsilon - 1) + wh' - \mu\varepsilon > 0$$

with $\quad \varepsilon \equiv \dfrac{-h''}{h'} c_1 \quad \mu \equiv \dfrac{\alpha}{c_1} \quad$ and as before $\quad \lambda \equiv \dfrac{c_2}{c_1}$. $\qquad$ (4.14)

Provided that the individual has no non-wage income, i.e. $\alpha = 0$, $\varepsilon > 1$ is a sufficient condition for the saving rate to increase with income. Accordingly, the marginal attractiveness of current consumption as a result of the efficiency and wage increasing effect must fall sufficiently rapidly.[124]

4.3 The importance of productive consumption for growth

4.3.1 Productive consumption enhances the stock of human capital*

4.3.1.1 The human-capital-enhancement function

The empirical studies which have been reviewed above clarify two essential points: (i) A rise in the level of nutrition, health efforts, and education increases the productive potential of labour. (ii) The marginal impact of nutrition, health efforts, and education on the productive potential of labour decreases with an increasing level of nutrition, health efforts, and education.[125]

Nutrition and health expenditures are clearly made in order to satisfy current needs and can be classified as consumption; in the case of education, this does not follow unambiguously. In fact, a considerable part of educational activities may not be considered as pure pleasure and is probably conceived as a traditional investment activity.[126]

---

* This section is based on Steger (2000b).

[123] As before, an isoelastic utility function and an interest rate equal to zero is supposed (Gersovitz, 1983, p. 850).

[124] For further interpretations see Gersovitz (1983, p. 850).

[125] Both propositions must be slightly qualified in the case of education (see Section 4.2.1).

[126] Recent growth models, which explain labour supply endogenously, interpret education as satisfying needs indirectly. In addition to consumption, the utility function contains 'leisure in efficiency units' as the product of leisure and the individual stock of human capital as an argument (Ladrón-de-Guevara, Ortigueira, and Santos, 1997, pp.130). Moreover, see Lazear (1977), who analyses theoretically and empirically the question whether education should be regarded as a production or consumption process.

To analyse the implications of productive consumption in the context of growth, the productive consumption effect is interpreted as enhancing the stock of human capital. This crucial hypothesis is specified in the form of a *'human-capital-enhancement function'*. In its intensive form, this concave and twice continuously differentiable function reads:

$$\dot{h}(t) = \phi[c(t)] - (n+\delta)h(t) \quad \text{with} \quad \phi'(c) > 0 \text{ and } \phi''(c) < 0. \tag{4.15}$$

All variables are expressed in per capita terms, t represents the time index, and a dot above a variable denotes its derivative with respect to time, i.e. $\dot{x}(t) \equiv dx(t)/dt$. In this case $h(t)$ denotes the stock of human capital at time t, $c(t)$ consumption, δ the depreciation rate of human capital, and n the population growth rate, respectively.[127] Equation (4.15) represents the equation of motion of the average stock of human capital. As a result of productive consumption, the stock of human capital increases according to the function $\phi[c(t)]$, while it decreases due to depreciation and population growth. Consequently, $\phi[c(t)]$ can be designated as the gross human-capital-enhancement function. The positive, but decreasing marginal human-capital-enhancement effect of consumption, $\phi'(c) > 0$ and $\phi''(c) < 0$, appears justified by the empirical evidence. The 'smooth' shape may not be reasonable at an individual level. However, this assumption hardly appears problematic at an aggregate level, i.e. if (4.15) is interpreted as average human-capital-enhancement function.

On account of its static character, traditional efficiency wage theory was forced to assume that consumption increases the efficiency of labour without any delay. In contrast, equation (4.15) indicates that productive consumption enhances the stock of human capital in the subsequent period. The human-capital-enhancement function (4.15) states that human capital is created exclusively as a result of productive consumption. Consequently, formal education as far as it represents an investment decision and learning-by-doing effects are ignored. The representation of productive consumption effects together with, for example, formal education is naturally possible within a comprehensive production function for human capital:

$$\dot{h}(t) = B[1-u(t)]h(t) + \phi[c(t)] - (\delta + n)h(t), \tag{4.16}$$

[127] To the best of my knowledge, the only model which postulates consumption to be productive in the sense of increasing the stock of human capital is Becker and Murphy (1988), though they call it 'consumption capital'. Within this framework, which aims at explaining addiction as the result of rational decisions over time, past consumption affects current utility through a process of 'learning by doing' (Becker and Murphy, 1988, p. 677).

where the first term on the right-hand side corresponds to the production function for human capital according to the Uzawa-Lucas model (Lucas, 1988, p. 18).

Several authors have recently incorporated a subsistence level of consumption into growth models by means of Stone-Geary preferences (Rebelo, 1992; Ben-David, 1994; Easterly, 1994; and Sarel, 1994). The subsistence level of consumption can be considered as representing the minimum gross enhancement of human capital in order to replace depreciation.[128] The differences between the concept of subsistence consumption and the human-capital-enhancement function are as follows: First, the former represents a modification of standard preference formulation while the latter represents a modification of technological opportunities. Second, the human-capital-enhancement function continuously accounts for productive consumption effects beyond the subsistence level.

The hypothesis of productive consumption in the form of equation (4.15) is not an assumption which serves primarily for abstraction, i.e. reducing the complexity of the real world. It rather constitutes a crucial assumption for the growth model presented in the next section, which focuses on important aspects of capital accumulation and growth in DCs.

4.3.1.2 The human-capital model

The linear growth model (Romer, 1986; Barro, 1990; Jones and Manuelli, 1990; and Rebelo, 1991) is a fairly simple endogenous growth model. It shows very clearly the conditions for permanent growth as well as the main implications of the endogenous growth theory. Permanent growth requires constant returns to scale in the factors that can be accumulated as well as a sufficiently high marginal productivity of these factors.[129] The long-run growth rate is determined by technology and preference parameters and hence internationally different parameter values can potentially explain internationally diverging growth experiences. A special feature of the linear growth model with constant-intertemporal-elasticity-of-substitution (CIES) preferences is that balanced-growth equilibrium is realised at any point in time, i.e. transitional dynamics cannot occur. In this section, a linear growth model which is extended by productive consumption is presented in general form using continuous time notation.

The representative household has access to a one-sector production technology with capital, $k(t)$, as the only input which is employed to pro-

---

[128] Fogel (1994, p. 372) reports estimates of daily calorie requirements to cover the baseline maintenance (the energy to keep the body functioning, i.e. basal metabolism plus energy for digestion of food and vital hygiene) for American males in the 18th century.

[129] For a derivation of the general conditions of permanent growth see Jones and Manuelli (1997).

duce an output good, $y(t)$, that can be used universally for investment or consumption purposes. The production function in its intensive form reads:

$$y(t) = f[k(t)] \quad \text{with} \quad f(0) = 0 \quad \text{and} \quad f'(k) = const. \tag{4.17}$$

The production function is linear homogeneous, i.e. the marginal productivity of the sole input is constant. The absence of diminishing returns is crucial for the generation of endogenous growth and can be justified mainly by two interpretations: First, capital is thought to exhibit positive spill-over effects or, second, capital can be interpreted broadly. Following this second interpretation, capital is defined to encompass physical as well as human capital. In addition, both types of capital can be additively aggregated if they are assumed to be perfect substitutes in production:

$$k(t) = k_p(t) + k_h(t). \tag{4.18}$$

Physical capital, $k_p(t)$, increases as a consequence of the renunciation of consumption, taking into account the rate of depreciation, δ, and the rate of population growth, n:

$$\dot{k}_p(t) = f[k(t)] - (n + \delta)k_p(t) - c(t). \tag{4.19}$$

Human capital, $k_h(t)$, is formed exclusively by productive consumption; the equation of motion for human capital equals the human-capital-enhancement function:

$$\dot{k}_h(t) = \phi[c(t)] - (n + \delta)k_h(t). \tag{4.20}$$

The gross human-capital-enhancement function, $\phi[c(t)]$, is assumed to be strictly concave and twice continuously differentiable with asymptotically vanishing first and second derivative:

$$\phi'(c) > 0 \quad \phi''(c) < 0 \quad \lim_{c \to \infty} \phi'(c) = 0 \quad \text{and} \quad \lim_{c \to \infty} \phi''(c) = 0. \tag{4.21}$$

Even though k_p is called physical capital and k_h is called human capital, from a formal point of view, the key distinction between the two types of capital is that k_p is produced on the basis of the same technology which is used to produce consumption goods and its accumulation necessarily requires, at least in part, the renunciation of consumption while k_h results from (productive) consumption. In this respect k_p could equally be interpreted as physical and human capital which requires the renunciation of consumption for its accumulation.

Using the simplifying assumption of identical depreciation rates, the equation of motion for the whole stock of capital reads according to (4.18) as follows:

$$\dot{k}(t) = f[k(t)] - (n + \delta)k(t) - \psi[c(t)]$$

with $\quad \psi[c(t)] \equiv c(t) - \phi[c(t)].$ $\qquad\qquad$ (4.22)

Usually, consumption is costly because it fully reduces net investments, i.e. the accumulation of (physical) capital. In the present context, consumption contributes to the accumulation of capital because it enhances the stock of human capital according to $\phi(c)$. Consequently, the *net cost of consumption* (NCC) in terms of forgone capital accumulation as a result of consumption are shown by $\psi(c)$. The NCC consists in consumption, i.e. forgone accumulation of (physical) capital, less the human-capital-enhancement effect of consumption.[130]

The representative household is assumed to maximise its dynastic lifetime utility. The corresponding dynamic optimisation problem is a concave, infinite time problem of optimal control with one control, $c(t)$, and one state variable, $k(t)$, as well as a bounded control set:

$$\max_{\{c(t)\}} \int_0^\infty u[c(t)] \cdot e^{-(\rho-n)\cdot t} \, dt$$

s.t. $\quad \dot{k}(t) = f[k(t)] - (\delta + n)k(t) - \psi[c(t)]$

$\qquad k(0) = k_0 \qquad k(t) \geq 0$

$\qquad 0 \leq c(t) \leq f[k(t)],$ $\qquad\qquad$ (4.23)

where $c(t)$ denotes consumption at time t, $u[c(t)]$ the instantaneous utility function, ρ the individual time preference rate, and n the constant growth rate of population, respectively. The instantaneous utility function is assumed to be strictly concave, $u'(c) > 0$ and $u''(c) < 0$, and to possess a constant elasticity of marginal utility with respect to consumption, $\sigma \equiv -u''(c)c / u'(c)$, i.e. a constant intertemporal elasticity of substitution, σ^{-1}.

The marginal NCC, $\psi'(c) = 1 - \phi'(c)$, is negative as long as the marginal human-capital-enhancement effect of consumption, $\phi'(c)$, is greater than unity. In this case, it clearly makes no sense to refrain from consumption and hence saving must be zero. Moreover, rational individuals would try to dissave whenever this possibility arises. But since only human capital has been accumulated in the past and the transformation of human

---

[130] The concept of NCC appears to be crucial within the underlying framework. I thank Karl-Josef Koch for suggesting the clarifying expression 'net cost of consumption'.

capital into consumption goods seems to be impossible, the (state-dependent) inequality constraint on the control variable, $c \le f(k)$, must be imposed and will turn out to be effectively binding at early stages of economic development.

The Lagrangian and the current-value Hamiltonian for the dynamic optimisation problem (4.23) read as follows:[131]

$$L(c,k,\lambda,v_1,v_2) = H(c,k,\lambda) + v_1[f(k)-c] + v_2 c \qquad (4.24)$$

$$H(c,k,\lambda) = u(c) + \lambda[f(k) - (\delta + n)k - \psi(c)] . \qquad (4.25)$$

The Hamiltonian (4.25), which represents the contribution of current output allocated to consumption and investment to overall benefit, illustrates the 'dual welfare effect' of consumption. The first part shows the direct contribution to utility, $u(c)$. As already mentioned, productive consumption reduces the NCC, $\psi(c)$, according to the human-capital-enhancement effect of consumption, $\phi(c)$. The second part of the Hamiltonian, which shows the net increase in the capital stock evaluated at the current-value shadow price, λ, captures this mechanism.[132]

The application of the maximum principle leads to the first-order conditions, where v_1 and v_2 denote the dynamic Lagrangian multipliers associated with each of the inequality constraints stated in (4.23):[133]

$$\frac{\partial L}{\partial \lambda} = \dot{k} = f(k) - (\delta + n)k - \psi(c) \qquad (4.26)$$

$$\dot{\lambda} = \lambda(\rho - n) - \frac{\partial L}{\partial k} = \lambda[\rho + \delta - f'(k)] - v_1 f'(k) \qquad (4.27)$$

$$\frac{\partial L}{\partial c} = u'(c) - \lambda\psi'(c) - v_1 + v_2 = 0 \qquad (4.28)$$

---

[131] For a presentation of optimal control theory with bounded control sets, see Kamien and Schwartz (1981, Section 10). Especially for optimal control theory with state-dependent inequality constraints on the control variable, see Feichtinger and Hartl (1986, Chapter 6). In order to simplify the notation, the time index will be suppressed.

[132] For an economic interpretation of the maximum principle and the Hamiltonian see Dorfman (1969).

[133] Because the Hamiltonian is concave in the control and the state variable, the necessary conditions are also sufficient for a maximum. In addition to the first-order conditions, an optimal trajectory must satisfy the transversality condition: $\lim_{t \to \infty} e^{-(\rho-n)\cdot t} \lambda(t)k_p(t) = 0$.

Notice that the transversality condition only applies to capital which results from the renunciation of consumption, i.e. physical capital.

$$v_1 \geq 0 \qquad v_1[f(k) - c] = 0 \tag{4.29}$$

$$v_2 \geq 0 \qquad v_2 c = 0. \tag{4.30}$$

4.3.1.3 Implications

The first-order conditions stated above indicate that boundary solutions have to be distinguished from interior solutions. Furthermore, interior solutions comprise the transition process to the asymptotic balanced-growth equilibrium and the asymptotic balanced-growth equilibrium itself. In order to illustrate the implications of the linear growth model with productive consumption, three 'ranges' are distinguished: (i) The no-saving range; (ii) the transition range; and the (iii) asymptotic range.

No-saving range

The first-order conditions (4.28), (4.29), and (4.30) imply a boundary solution with $c = f(k)$ if the following weak inequality holds:

$$u'(c) \geq \lambda \psi'(c). \tag{4.31}$$

As long as marginal utility of consumption exceeds the marginal NCC measured in units of utility, an increase in consumption approaching the upper limit of the control set, $k \geq 0$ and $0 \leq c \leq f(k)$, appears rational and saving is zero.

Within the no-saving range the evolution of the economy is determined by the equation of motion for capital (4.22), taking into account that saving is zero:

$$\dot{k} = \phi[f(k)] - (\delta + n)k. \tag{4.32}$$

It should be observed that an increase in overall capital is possible in the present model although the saving rate is zero. As a consequence of the properties of the human-capital-enhancement function, the differential equation in the capital stock (4.32) possesses a stable equilibrium point whenever the sum of the depreciation rate and the population growth rate is positive. If the stationary value of capital lies inside the no-saving range, the economy runs into a *poverty trap*: Individuals do not save during this early stage of economic development and no physical capital is accumulated. However, human capital is created as a consequence of productive consumption activities. Because of the diminishing marginal human-capital-enhancement effect of consumption, the net human capital accumulation decreases and may approach zero before the end of the no-saving range is reached and the accumulation of physical capital sets in.[134]

The growth rates of consumption and output equal the growth rate of capital:

$$\frac{\dot{c}}{c} = \frac{\dot{y}}{y} = \frac{\dot{k}}{k} = \frac{\phi[f(k)]}{k} - (\delta + n). \tag{4.33}$$

The growth rate of consumption in (4.33) is independent of preferences. Hence, the intertemporal elasticity of substitution (IES) is effectively zero within the no-saving range.

Transition range

The first-order conditions (4.28), (4.29), and (4.30) imply an interior solution, $0 < c < y$, provided that the following equality holds: [135]

$$u'(c) = \lambda\psi'(c). \tag{4.34}$$

As soon as the marginal utility of consumption equals the marginal NCC measured in units of utility, the optimal trajectory leaves the boundary and runs into the interior of the open control set; provided that the poverty trap did not become binding. Along the optimal trajectory, equality (4.34) holds as a necessary optimum condition. The comparison of (4.34) with the usual optimum condition, $u'(c) = \lambda$, taking into account the definition of the marginal NCC, $\psi'(c) = 1 - \phi'(c)$, and the concavity of the utility function, indicates that the level of consumption is higher than in a situation without productive consumption effects, as one would expect.

Differentiation of equation (4.34) with respect to time, subsequently dividing the result by the original relation (4.34), eliminating the shadow price using equation (4.27), and noting that v_1 is zero for an interior solution yields the optimal growth rate of consumption:

$$\frac{\dot{c}}{c} = [\sigma - \eta(c)]^{-1} \cdot [f'(k) - \delta - \rho]$$

---

[134] The possibility of a poverty trap even opens up within the framework of an endogenous growth model. One can expect that productive consumption within a neoclassical model increases the probability of a poverty trap.

[135] The third possibility of $c = 0$ would require $u'(c) \le \lambda\psi'(c)$. On account of the characteristics of the utility and human-capital-enhancement functions and a positive shadow price of capital, the case of $c = 0$ does not emerge.

with $\eta(c) \equiv -\dfrac{c\psi''(c)}{\psi'(c)} = \dfrac{c\phi''(c)}{1-\phi'(c)} \leq 0$. [136] $\qquad(4.35)$

The evolution of the economy in the case of interior solutions is governed by the differential equations in consumption, (4.22), and capital, (4.35). The second expression of the denominator on the right-hand side of (4.35) denotes the *elasticity of the marginal NCC* with respect to consumption, $\eta(c)$. Corresponding to the nature of the human-capital-enhancement function, $\eta(c)$ is negative while its absolute value decreases with an increasing level of consumption and asymptotically approaches zero.

Equation (4.35) is the *modified Keynes-Ramsey rule* of optimal consumption. The ratio on the right-hand side can be designated as *effective IES*, eIES. It is worth noting that the eIES is not exclusively determined by the instantaneous utility function but that it is additionally dependent on the technological possibilities to enhance the stock of human capital as a result of productive consumption. The eIES expresses the willingness to substitute consumption intertemporally, taking into account a change in the marginal utility as well as a change in the marginal NCC. According to (4.35), the eIES and the growth rate of consumption increase along the (infinite) transition to the asymptotic balanced-growth equilibrium.

With respect to (4.35), one could argue that productive consumption has no impact on growth rates provided that the human-capital-enhancement function implies a constant elasticity of the marginal NCC; analogous to the use of CIES utility functions. The class of human-capital-enhancement functions which give rise to a constant elasticity of the marginal NCC is of the following form (see Appendix 4-1):

$$\phi(c) = c - \frac{a_1}{1-\eta}c^{1-\eta} + a_2,\qquad(4.36)$$

where a_1 and a_2 are some positive constants and η denotes the (constant) elasticity of the marginal NCC. However, it can be shown that (4.36) cannot fulfil the requirements of $\phi'(c) > 0$ and $\phi''(c) < 0$, stated in (4.21). In addition, the conventional case of consumption inducing no productive effects at all can be considered as a special case with $a_1 = 1$, $a_2 = 0$, and $\eta = 0$.

---

[136] The validity of the so-called growth condition $f'(k) > \rho + \delta$ is assumed. Equation (4.35) is only valid for an interior solution, where the marginal NCC must be smaller than unity. Consequently, the denominator of $\eta(c)$ cannot become negative and $\eta(c)$ is well defined.

In order to give a clear economic interpretation of the modified Keynes-Ramsey rule, equation (4.35) is slightly reworded to:

$$f'(k) = \rho + \delta - \underbrace{\frac{u''(c)\dot{c}}{u'(c)}}_{<0\,for\,\dot{c}>0} + \underbrace{\frac{\psi''(c)\dot{c}}{\psi'(c)}}_{>0\,for\,\dot{c}>0}. \qquad (4.37)$$

The third term on the right-hand side of (4.37) is the percentage time rate of change of the marginal utility which represents 'the psychic cost of saving' (Dorfmann, 1969, p. 825). The last term on the right-hand side is the percentage time rate of change of the marginal NCC. Holding an additional unit of capital during a short interval of time causes a rising consumption profile and induces a rise in the marginal NCC. Along the optimal path the rate of consumption must be chosen so that the marginal productivity of capital covers four components: the time preference rate, the depreciation rate, the psychic cost of saving, and additionally the rise in the marginal NCC.[137]

The saving rate is zero at the beginning of the transition process and can be shown to converge asymptotically towards a positive constant, which equals the saving rate of the original linear growth model [see Appendix 4-2 and Section 4.3.1.4, Fig. 4.2 (c) and (d)].

What about the growth rate of income? Whether it decreases or increases seems not to be unequivocal *a priori*. Differentiation of the growth rate of income with respect to time yields:

$$\frac{d}{dt}\frac{\dot{k}}{k} = \frac{d}{dt}\frac{\phi(c)}{k} - \frac{d}{dt}\frac{c}{k}. \qquad (4.38)$$

The first term on the right-hand side of (4.38) is closely related to the time rate of change of the growth rate of human capital, while the second term is closely related to the time rate of change of the growth rate of physical capital. The transition process is illustrated, at least for a specific set of parameters, in Section 4.3.1.4.

Asymptotic range

The linear growth model with productive consumption does not possess a balanced-growth equilibrium defined by constant growth rates. Nonetheless, balanced growth occurs as an asymptotic property, i.e. in the interior of the control region the optimal trajectory converges asymptotically towards a balanced-growth path, along which the growth rates of the endogenous variables are constant. Hence, the optimal trajectory is called an *asymptotic balanced-growth path*, denoted by BGP^∞. The balanced-

---

[137] For an economic interpretation of the Keynes-Ramsey rule see Dorfman (1969, p. 825).

growth path, which is a ray in the present case, describes the (asymptotic) direction of the BGP^∞ and is denoted by $DBGP^\infty$ (Koch, 1999). In order to describe the asymptotic behaviour of the extended linear growth model, consider the growth rate of capital as time approaches infinity and consumption and capital grow without bounds:

$$\lim_{t\to\infty}\frac{\dot{k}}{k} = f'(k) - \delta - n - \lim_{t\to\infty}\frac{c}{k} + \lim_{t\to\infty}\frac{\phi(c)}{k}. \tag{4.39}$$

The last term on the right-hand side of (4.39) eventually vanishes [see equation (A.4.7) in Appendix 4-2]. With respect to the relation between the asymptotic growth rate of consumption, $\gamma_c{}^*$, and the asymptotic growth rate of capital, $\gamma_k{}^*$, three cases can be distinguished: (i) $\gamma_c{}^* < \gamma_k{}^*$; (ii) $\gamma_c{}^* > \gamma_k{}^*$; and (iii) $\gamma_c{}^* = \gamma_k{}^*$.

In the case of (i), equation (4.39) implies an asymptotic growth rate of capital equal to $f'(k) - \delta - n$. However, this would violate a necessary optimum condition, the transversality condition (stated in footnote 61).[138] In case (ii), equation (4.39) formally implies that the growth rate of capital tends to minus infinity. In fact, the trajectory would hit the boundary of the admissible control set and would subsequently run into the poverty trap. This can obviously not be optimal as well. The only remaining possibility is case (iii) with $\gamma_c{}^* = \gamma_k{}^*$, i.e. the growth rates of consumption and capital have the same limit as time approaches infinity. Taking further into account the disappearance of the elasticity of the marginal NCC as time approaches infinity, equation (4.35) shows the asymptotic growth rate of consumption. The relation $\gamma_c{}^* = \gamma_k{}^*$ together with the production function (4.17) imply that all endogenous variables, i.e. consumption, capital, and income, grow asymptotically with the same growth rate:[139]

---

[138] Because physical capital accumulation is a linear function in output and human capital accumulation is a sub-linear function in output, the portion of physical capital to overall capital asymptotically approaches unity. Consequently, the asymptotic growth rate of physical capital equals the right-hand side of (4.39), ignoring the last term. The transversality condition forces the stock of physical capital per capita to grow asymptotically with a rate smaller than $f'(k) - \delta - n$. To see this, note that the transversality condition can be written as $\lim_{t\to\infty}\lambda(\tau)e^{-[f'(k)-\delta-n]\cdot t}k_p(t) = 0$, where τ denotes the point in time when an interior solution occurs for the first time (Barro and Sala-i-Martin, 1995, pp. 167-169).

[139] The production function is assumed to be sufficiently productive to guarantee permanent growth, and overall utility is assumed to be bounded. This requires: $f'(k) - \delta > \rho > [(1-\sigma)/\sigma]\cdot[f'(k) - \delta - \rho] + n$ (Barro and Sala-i-Martin, 1995, p. 142).

$$\lim_{t \to \infty} \frac{\dot{c}}{c} = \lim_{t \to \infty} \frac{\dot{k}}{k} = \lim_{t \to \infty} \frac{\dot{y}}{y} = \sigma^{-1}\left[f'(k) - \delta - \rho\right]. \qquad (4.40)$$

In summary, Fig. 4.1 sketches the phase diagram of the extended linear growth model. The two rays starting from the origin represent the production function and the $DBGP^{\infty}$, respectively. The curve starting on the vertical axis for $c > 0$ describes the $\dot{k} = 0$-locus.[140] The horizontal broken line marks that level of consumption for which the marginal human-capital-enhancement effect of consumption equals unity. The region below this line necessarily belongs to the no-saving range and the dynamic evolution of the economy is governed by (4.40) and $c = f(k)$. Starting with an initial stock of capital, $k(0)$, which is chosen sufficiently small to give rise to a boundary solution initially, the corresponding level of consump

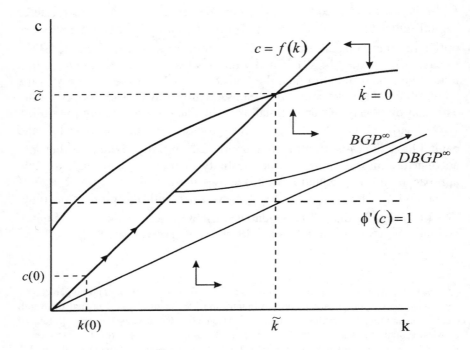

Fig. 4.1. Phase diagram of the linear growth model with productive consumption

---

[140] The shape of the $\dot{k} = 0$-locus in Fig. 4.1 is based on the specific functions employed for the simulation (Section 4.3.1.4). Technically, the $\dot{k} = 0$-locus runs through the second quadrant and enters into the first quadrant whenever there is a range of c for which $\phi(c) > c$. However, according to (4.23) the stock of capital is defined of the range $k \geq 0$.

tion, $c(0)$, is located on the boundary of the control set. The optimal trajectory moves along the production function to the north-east and enters
into the control region as soon as the marginal utility of consumption
equals the marginal NCC measured in units of utility. However, if this
critical point is located in the north-east of the poverty trap coordinates
$(\tilde{c}, \tilde{k})$, the economy would run into a poverty trap. Provided that the poverty trap did not become binding, the optimal trajectory, i.e. the BGP^{∞},
enters into the control region and converges asymptotically to the
$DBGP^{\infty}$, which equals the BGP of the linear model.

4.3.1.4 Simulation results

In order to illustrate the transitional dynamics of the model, at least for a
specific set of functions and parameters, the transition process for an interior solution is simulated. That is, the system of differential equations
(4.22) and (4.35) is approximated numerically by means of the subroutine
NDSolve of Mathematica®. The following functions and parameter values
have been employed: $u(c) = \dfrac{c^{1-\theta} - 1}{1-\theta}$, $f(k) = Ak$, $\phi(c) = c^{\beta}$, $A = 0.1$,
$\theta = 3$, $\delta = 0.02$, $\rho = 0.01$, $n = 0.03$, and $\beta = 0.05$ ($\beta = 0.35$).[141] [142]

Fig. 4.2 (a) to (f) shows the time paths of the elasticity of the marginal
NCC, $\eta(t)$, the effective intertemporal elasticity of substitution, $eIES(t)$,
the saving rate, $s(t)$, the saving function, $s(y)$, the time paths of the
growth rate of capital, $grk(t)$, and the consumption-capital ratio,
$c(t)/k(t)$, respectively. Several points are worth being emphasised.

First of all, all variables converge monotonically towards their asymptotic balanced-growth-equilibrium values. The average rate of convergence
measured on the basis of the consumption-capital ratio according to
$\lambda = -\ln[(x(t) - x*)/(x(0) - x*)]/t$ reads $\lambda \cong -\ln(0.5)/15 \cong 0.046$. The
broken line in Fig. 4.2 (f) shows the time path of the consumption-capital

---

[141] The use of a gross human-capital-enhancement function which is bounded from above,
e.g. $\phi(c) = Bc/(B+c)$, does not alter the simulation results qualitatively.

[142] The initial conditions are determined as follows: First, an arbitrary but sufficiently high
value of capital per capita is selected. The value of per capita consumption is chosen to be
located on the asymptotic balanced-growth path. Second, starting from this point the system
is solved backwards. Third, the resulting trajectory passes through the boundary of the
control set; this point of intersection is used as the starting point of the forward solution.
The initial values of the backward solution are sufficiently high in the following sense:
Multiplying these values by two and following the same procedure does not alter the time
paths of the Fig. 4.2 on inspection.

ratio for $\beta = 0.35$. The speed of convergence in this case amounts to $\lambda \cong -\ln(0.5)/20 \cong 0.035$. Therefore, the speed of convergence appears to be inversely related to the efficiency of the human-capital-enhancement process. A possible economic reasoning for this result is as follows: The higher the marginal human-capital-enhancement effect of consumption, the stronger is the bias against saving. Because the marginal human-capital-enhancement effect of consumption is smaller than unity for interior solutions, the accumulation of (physical and human) capital is smaller on balance.

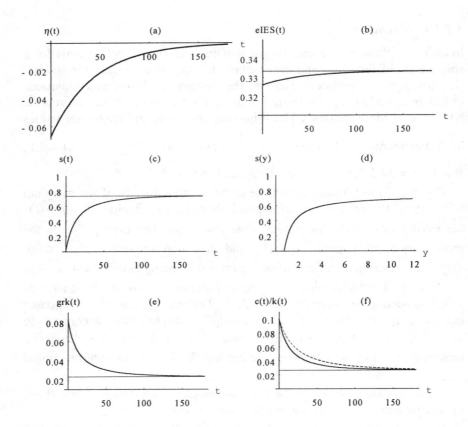

Fig. 4.2. Simulation results for the human-capital model

Second, the growth rate of capital and thus income decreases during the transition process [Fig. 4.2 (e)]. This result is somewhat surprising because a rising saving rate [Fig. 4.2 (c)] induces two effects on the growth rate of capital: (i) As time proceeds a rising portion of output (saving rate) is used for gross physical capital investment, and (ii) a falling portion of output (consumption rate) can be used for gross human-capital enhancements due to productive consumption. As the marginal human-capital-enhancement effect of consumption is smaller than unity for interior solutions, one would at first glance expect that effect (i) dominates effect (ii). However, (4.38) indicates that the crucial point is whether the time rate of change of the human capital component exceeds the time rate of change of the physical capital component. Obviously, Fig. 4.2 (e) shows that in the present case the time rate of change of the human capital component dominates the time rate of change of the physical capital component. Hence, the model implies (conditional) ß-convergence together with a rising saving rate.

Third, King and Rebelo (1993, p. 908) point to a well-known quantitative problem of the neoclassical growth model: "Generally, when one tries to explain sustained economic growth with transitional dynamics, there are extremely counterfactual implications. These result from the fact that implied marginal products are extraordinarily high in the early stages of development." [143] The extended linear growth model with productive consumption does not bear this implication. Sustained economic growth with transitional dynamics is compatible with a constant marginal product of the reproducible factors.

Fourth, Fig. 4.2 (a) shows the elasticity of the marginal NCC, which is negative and converges asymptotically towards zero. As a consequence, the eIES is low at early stages of economic development, increases and asymptotically approaches a constant. In addition, for boundary solutions the IES is effectively zero [see equation (4.33)]. However, it should be noted that the variation of η is comparably small and the variation of the eIES is even smaller [Fig. 4.2 (b).[144] Several authors have reported empirical evidence in favour of IES-values which do not significantly differ from zero in the case of low-income countries (Giovannini, 1985) as well as empirical evidence in favour of a positive relation between the IES and per capita income (Atkeson and Ogaki, 1996 and Ogaki, Ostry, and Reinhart, 1996).[145] The present model implies a rising eIES during the transition due

---

[143] In addition see Mankiw (1995, pp. 286-289).

[144] This quantitative shortcoming does not appear within the labour-efficiency model discussed in the next section.

[145] The finding of a very low interest rate sensitivity of saving in a number of DCs has led several authors to consider a number of hypotheses that could explain this result. Mainly two hypotheses were employed: liquidity constraints and Stone-Geary preferences (Rebelo, 1992; Easterly, 1994; and Ogaki, Ostry, and Reinhart, 1996).

to the technological possibilities to enhance the stock of human capital as a result of productive consumption. From this one can potentially explain the negligible effects of structural adjustment policies with the objective to increase the real interest rate, encourage savings and foster economic growth in the case of low-income countries (Ogaki, Ostry, and Reinhart, 1996).

Fifth, Rebelo (1992) argues that an important shortcoming of a 'broad class of endogenous growth models' is that they cannot explain different growth experiences in the presence of international capital markets. Provided that some symmetry with respect to technology and preferences holds, all economies face the same real rate of return and exhibit the same growth rate of per capita income. After discussing several extensions of the basic linear growth model, Rebelo (1992, p. 27) concludes: "*In summary, with the exception of taxation under the worldwide system, the mechanisms described [...] do not survive as sources of growth differentials in the presence of international capital markets.*" [146] The linear growth model with productive consumption shows transitional dynamics which survive international capital markets and identical real rates of return.

Sixth, as Fig. 4.2 (d) demonstrates, the (gross) saving rate increases from zero at the beginning of the transition and converges towards its asymptotic balanced-growth value. The economic reason is simply that productive consumption reduces the marginal NCC. As a result, a bias against saving occurs which is especially marked at low levels of consumption and vanishes asymptotically. The rising time path of the saving rate in turn implies a saving function which is positively sloped as Fig. 4.2 (d) illustrates. The empirical evidence in favour of a positive correlation between the saving rate and the level of per capita income is overwhelming.[147] As an illustration of the cross-country data consider Table 2.1 in Section 2.1. The figures show that the largest increase occurs with the transition from low-income to lower middle-income countries. Obviously, the relation between the saving rate and the level of per capita income is non-linear which is in line with Fig. 4.2 (d).

Finally, Fig. 4.3 illustrates the saddle-point stability of the BGP^{∞} based on the same functions and parameter values which have been employed for the simulation.

---

[146] Rebelo (1992) suggests a modification of the standard CIES preferences into Stone-Geary preferences to solve this theoretical problem.

[147] See Thirlwall (1974, Chapter 7) for a review of the older and Reichel (1993) for a review of the more recent literature. In addition, see Rebelo (1992) and Ogaki, Ostry, and Reinhart (1996).

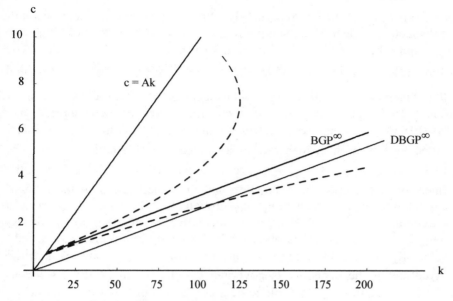

Fig. 4.3. Illustration of (infinite) saddle-point stability

The figure shows the upper boundary of the control set, $c = Ak$, and the $DBGP^\infty$. In addition, it contains one stable trajectory, the BGP^∞, and two instable trajectories, which are shown by the broken lines. The BGP^∞ starts at the turning point, which is the beginning of the stable arm of the saddle path and converges towards the $DBGP^\infty$. The two instable trajectories start on the border of the control set slightly above or below the turning point. The trajectory which starts above the turning point eventually curves back and hits the boundary of the admissible control set. The other trajectory which starts below the stable arm of the saddle path sooner or later crosses the $DBGP^\infty$ and converges towards the horizontal axes.

4.3.1.5 Modifications

The hypothesis of productive consumption specified by the human-capital-enhancement function represents the crucial element of the model discussed above. This section seeks to investigate concisely the implications which result from two plausible modifications of the human-capital-enhancement function.

First, similarly to the specification of the effort function employed within the efficiency wage literature, the gross human-capital-enhancement function, $\phi(c)$, can be assumed to show a mixed convex-concave shape (e.g. Gersovitz, 1983). Accordingly, the marginal gross human-capital-enhancement effect of consumption increases for low values of consumption and decreases beyond a threshold level of consumption, i.e. $\phi'(c) > 0$, $\lim_{c \to \infty} \phi'(c) = 0$ (as before) and $\phi''(c) > 0 \forall c < \hat{c}$, $\phi''(c) < 0 \forall c > \hat{c}$. Provided that the marginal human-capital-enhancement effect of consumption is equal or bigger than unity at the initial level of consumption, i.e. $\phi'[c(0)] \geq 1$, a corner solution results definitely.[148] Within the no-saving range the common growth rate of all the original variables as stated in (4.33) reads $\phi[f(k)]k^{-1} - \delta - n$. Provided that $c(0) < \hat{c}$ it follows from the linearity of the production function and the specification of the human-capital-enhancement function that growth first accelerates, reaches a maximum at $c = \hat{c}$, and decelerates thereafter.[149] This non-monotonic dynamic of growth rate takes place while the saving rate remains zero. Subsequently, an interior solution occurs as soon as $u'(c) = \lambda \psi'(c)$ and the evolution of the economy is governed by (4.22) and (4.35). As it was shown above the transition-range necessarily requires that $\phi'(c) < 1$. Consequently, an interior solution can only occur within the concave region of the human-capital-enhancement function, i.e. for $c > \hat{c}$. The adjustment process towards the asymptotic balanced-growth equilibrium inside the transition range is qualitatively identical to the basic model.

Second, it might be reasonable to assume that the marginal gross human-capital-enhancement effect of consumption diminishes quickly rather than asymptotically and effectively becomes zero as soon as consumption approaches a threshold level. In this case the human-capital-enhancement function is characterised by $\phi'(c) > 0$, $\phi''(c) < 0 \quad \forall c < \hat{c}$ and $\phi'(c) = \phi''(c) = 0 \forall c \geq \hat{c}$. For the upper range $c \geq \hat{c}$ the human-capital-enhancement function reads $\phi(c) = a$ with a being a positive constant. The expression of the class of human-capital-enhancement functions characterised by a constant elasticity of the marginal NCC (4.36) shows that this specification represents a human-capital-enhancement function with an elasticity of the marginal NCC equal to zero, $\eta(c) = 0$ (for $c \geq \hat{c}$). As in a traditional context without productive effects of consumption, at $c = \hat{c}$ the marginal NCC becomes unity, i.e. $\psi'(c) = 1 \forall c \geq \hat{c}$. With respect to the first-order conditions (4.27) and (4.28) it is clear that an interior solution

---

[148] In fact $\phi'[c(0)] \geq 1$ is sufficient for a corner solution, however it is not necessary. The necessary and sufficient condition for a corner solution is: $u'[c(0)] \geq \lambda(0)\psi'[c(0)]$.

[149] See Easterly (1994) and the literature cited therein for the empirical phenomenon of a hump-shaped relation between the growth rate and the level of per capita income.

occurs.[150] In this case, the constant growth rate of consumption is given by
(4.35) noting that $\eta(c) = 0$, while (4.22) indicates the growth rate of capital. From the discussion of the linear growth model it is known that the
growth rate of capital would be equal to the growth rate of consumption if
$\phi(c) = 0$ (e.g. Barro and Sala-i-Martin, 1995, Chapter 4). However, with
$\phi(c) = a$ the growth rate of capital exceeds that of consumption by the
term a/k which vanishes asymptotically. Hence, the growth rate of capital
falls and approaches asymptotically its balanced-growth-equilibrium value
given by (4.40). The saving rate increases monotonically and approaches
asymptotically its balanced-growth-equilibrium value in the same way.

4.3.1.6 Summary and conclusion

Empirical evidence clearly indicates that productive inputs are not exclusively accumulated as a result of the renunciation of consumption. Especially at early stages of economic development, consumption can be regarded as a source of the accumulation of a productive input, i.e. human
capital, and hence output growth. The model presented above sheds some
light on the importance and implications of productive consumption, capital accumulation, and growth in DCs. Specifically, the incorporation of the
productive-consumption hypothesis into a simple endogenous growth
model reveals the following implications:

(1) The harsh intertemporal consumption trade-off traditionally assumed
    is modified. Specifically, the time rate of change of the marginal net
    cost of consumption has to be taken into account for selecting the op-
    timal consumption path. The optimal rule of consumption turns into a
    modified Keynes-Ramsey rule.
(2) The intertemporal elasticity of substitution is no longer based exclu-
    sively on the instantaneous utility function. The technological oppor-
    tunities to enhance the stock of human capital as a result of productive
    consumption additionally determine the effective IES (eIES). Conse-
    quently, the eIES consists in the elasticity of marginal utility as well
    as the elasticity of the marginal net cost of consumption.
(3) As Gersovitz (1983) has demonstrated within the framework of dis-
    crete two-period models, the saving rate increases with income if con-
    sumption is productive. In contrast to Gersovitz, this is shown within
    the framework of a continuous growth model and no special parameter
    restrictions are necessary for this result.

---

[150] The static and dynamic efficiency conditions [(4.28) and (4.27)] are identical to a situation without productive consumption. An interior solution must occur provided that the
parameters of the basic linear model are such that unbounded growth results.

(4) Different growth experiences are explained as the result of transitional dynamics towards an asymptotic balanced-growth equilibrium. The rate of convergence appears to be related inversely to the efficiency of the human-capital-enhancement process. The model does not imply unrealistically high values of the marginal product of reproducible factors for low incomes as most versions of the neoclassical growth model (King and Rebelo, 1993). Neither are identical real rates of return across economies due to international capital markets inconsistent with diverging growth rates for different countries (Rebelo, 1992).

Several extensions of the basic linear growth model with productive consumption are conceivable. The rate of population growth can be regarded as depending on the level of per capita consumption (Nelson, 1956). With respect to technology, it can be assumed that both types of capital, k_p and k_h, are essential for the production of output.[151] In addition, enhancements of human capital as a result of productive consumption can be incorporated into two-sector models of endogenous growth along the lines of Lucas (1988) and Rebelo (1991). Finally, productive consumption can be considered as increasing the efficiency of labour. This interpretation will be analysed within the following section.

4.3.2 Productive consumption increases the efficiency of labour

4.3.2.1 The labour-efficiency model

It is now assumed that productive consumption increases the efficiency of labour. The production technology employed in this model must therefore explicitly contain labour as a productive input. A natural starting point is the neoclassical production function. It is, however, assumed that the marginal product of capital is bounded sufficiently from below in order to guarantee unbounded growth.[152] The production function, which is assumed linearly homogenous in capital and labour, can be written in intensive form as: $y = f(k,c)$. This production function is equally consistent with the interpretation that productive consumption increases the efficiency of human capital. The main difference between the underlying interpretation and the human-capital model of the previous section is as follows: Productive consumption in this case is considered as increasing the efficiency of the whole stock of a productive input (labour or human capital), whereas productive consumption interpreted as enhancing the stock of

---

[151] Barro (1990) uses a linear homogenous production function where both private and government capital are essential for the production of output.

[152] This assumption is not crucial for the analysis, it merely means that the balanced-growth equilibrium rate of growth is positive.

human capital solely contributes to an increase in the stock of a productive input. From a formal point of view, the current formulation means that the production function is additionally dependent on consumption, whereas the interpretation employed within the previous model leads to a modified equation of motion of capital. In addition, the production function is assumed to satisfy the following conditions:

(i) $\dfrac{\partial f(k,c)}{\partial k} > 0$;   (ii) $\dfrac{\partial^2 f(k,c)}{\partial k^2} < 0$;   (iii) $\dfrac{\partial f(k,c)}{\partial c} > 0$;

(iv) $\dfrac{\partial^2 f(k,c)}{\partial c^2} < 0$; (v) $\dfrac{\partial^2 f(k,c)}{\partial k \partial c} > 0$; (vi) $\lim\limits_{c \to \infty} \dfrac{\partial f(k,c)}{\partial c} = 0$ for all k;

(vii) $\lim\limits_{c \to \infty} \dfrac{\partial^2 f(k,c)}{\partial k \partial c} = 0$ for all k; and (viii) $\lim\limits_{k \to \infty} \dfrac{\partial f(k,c)}{\partial k} = G > \delta + \rho$ for all c.

The conditions (i) and (ii) indicate a positive but falling marginal product of capital. Condition (iii) shows that output is positively related to consumption because the efficiency of labour is endogenously determined by the level of consumption (per capita). According to (iv) the strength of this effect falls with an increasing level of consumption. It should be noted explicitly that the marginal product of capital is positively related to the level of consumption as shown by (v). Lastly, the conditions (vi) to (viii) describe asymptotic properties: The marginal productive effect of consumption vanishes asymptotically as shown by (vi), the marginal product of capital cannot be increased indefinitely by increasing c as shown by (vii), and the asymptotic marginal product of capital is sufficiently bounded from below as indicated by (viii). As an example consider a modified Jones-Manuelli production function (Jones and Manuelli, 1990, pp. 1016/1017 and Jones and Manuelli, 1997, pp. 81/82) with the efficiency of labour being endogenously determined by the level of consumption: $y = [A(c)]^{1-\alpha} k^{\alpha} + Gk$ with $A(c) = Bc/(B+c)$. [153]

The dynamic optimisation problem faced by the representative household equals the dynamic optimisation problem characterised in (4.23) with two exceptions: (i) The equation of motion of capital now reads: $\dot{k} = f(k, c) - (\delta + n)k - c$. (ii) The admissible control set has the following shape: $0 \le c \le f(k,c)$.

---

[153] Another specific production function which satisfies the assumptions stated above is the CES production function with an elasticity of substitution greater than unity (Jones and Manuelli, 1997, pp. 81/82) and an efficiency of labour which is determined endogenously by consumption.

4.3.2.2 Implications

Dynamic optimisation within this setting implies the following first-order condition which has to be satisfied for an interior solution: [154]

$$u'(c) = \lambda \varphi(k,c) \qquad \text{with} \qquad \varphi(k,c) \equiv 1 - \frac{\partial f(k,c)}{\partial c}, \tag{4.41}$$

where $\varphi(k,c)$ can be similarly designated as the marginal NCC. Differentiation of (4.41) with respect to time, dividing by the original relation and eliminating the shadow price yields the modified Keynes-Ramsey rule of this model: [155]

$$\frac{\dot{c}}{c} = [\sigma - \varepsilon(k,c)]^{-1} \cdot \left[\frac{\partial f(k,c)}{\partial k} - \delta - \rho + \gamma(k,c) \frac{k}{k} \right]$$

with

$$\varepsilon(k,c) \equiv - \frac{\frac{\partial \varphi(k,c)}{\partial c} c}{\varphi(k,c)} = \frac{\frac{\partial^2 f(k,c)}{\partial c^2} c}{1 - \frac{\partial f(k,c)}{\partial c}} < 0$$

$$\gamma(k,c) \equiv - \frac{\frac{\partial \varphi(k,c)}{\partial k} k}{\varphi(k,c)} = \frac{\frac{\partial^2 f(k,c)}{\partial c \partial k} k}{1 - \frac{\partial f(k,c)}{\partial c}} > 0, \tag{4.42}$$

where $\varepsilon(k,c)$ denotes the partial elasticity of the marginal NCC with respect to consumption and $\gamma(k,c)$ denotes the partial elasticity of the marginal NCC with respect to capital. In order to give a clear economic interpretation of this modified Keynes-Ramsey rule, equation (4.42) is slightly reworded to:

---

[154] Because the Hamiltonian of the underlying dynamic problem is concave in the control and the state variable, the necessary conditions are also sufficient for a maximum. In addition to the first-order conditions, an optimal trajectory must satisfy the transversality condition: $\lim_{t \to \infty} e^{-(\rho-n)\cdot t} \lambda(t)k(t) = 0$.

[155] Equation (4.42) is only valid for interior solutions, where $\varphi(k,c)$ must be smaller than unity. Consequently, the denominator of $\varepsilon(k,c)$ and $\gamma(k,c)$ is well defined. See Appendix 4-4 for a derivation of the first-order conditions and the modified Keynes-Ramsey rule.

$$
\underbrace{\frac{\partial f(k,c)}{\partial k} - \frac{\dfrac{\partial \varphi(k,c) \dot{k}}{\partial k}}{\varphi(k,c)}}_{<0\,for\,\dot{k}>0} = \rho + \delta - \frac{u''(c)\dot{c}}{u'(c)} + \underbrace{\frac{\dfrac{\partial \varphi(k,c) \dot{c}}{\partial c}}{\varphi(k,c)}}_{>0\,for\,\dot{c}>0}. \tag{4.43}
$$

The second expression on the left-hand side of (4.43) shows the percentage time rate of change of the marginal NCC due to an increase in the stock of capital, while the last term on the right-hand side of (4.43) shows the percentage time rate of change of the marginal NCC resulting from an increase in the level of consumption. Holding an additional unit of capital during a short interval of time causes two kinds of marginal benefits, which appear on the left of (4.43): The marginal return from capital accumulation and, additionally, the decrease in the marginal NCC. On the other hand, analogous to the human-capital model discussed in the previous section, a rising consumption profile induces marginal cost which appears on the right of (4.43). Along the optimal path the rate of consumption at each moment must be chosen such that the marginal productivity of capital together with the decrease in the marginal NCC due to $\dot{k} > 0$ covers the time preference rate, the depreciation rate, 'the psychic cost of saving', and the rise in the marginal NCC due to $\dot{c} > 0$.

Provided that $\varepsilon(k,c)$ and $\gamma(k,c)$ converge to zero as c and k converge to infinity and the marginal product of capital is sufficiently bounded from below, the model under study possesses an asymptotic balanced-growth equilibrium characterised by $\lim\limits_{t \to \infty} \dfrac{\dot{c}}{c} = \lim\limits_{t \to \infty} \dfrac{\dot{k}}{k} = \sigma^{-1}(G - \delta - \rho)$,

where σ^{-1} denotes the constant IES.[156]

4.3.2.3 Simulation results

In order to illustrate the transitional dynamics of the labour-efficiency model, the differential equation in c together with the equation of motion of capital is approximated numerically. The following functions and set of parameters have been employed: $u(c) = \dfrac{c^{1-\theta} - 1}{1 - \theta}$, $y = \left(\dfrac{Bc}{B+c}\right)^{1-\alpha} k^\alpha + Gk$,

$B = 0.1$, $G = 0.1$, $\alpha = 0.3$, $\theta = 3$, $\delta = 0.02$, $\rho = 0.01$, and $n = 0.03$. Fig. 4.4 shows the time paths of the partial elasticity of the marginal NCC with respect to consumption, $\varepsilon(t)$, the effective intertemporal elasticity of

---

[156] See Appendix 4-5 for the proof of stability of the asymptotic balanced-growth equilibrium.

substitution, $eIES(t)$, the saving rate, $s(t)$, the consumption-capital ratio, $c(t)/k(t)$, the growth rate of output, $gry(t)$, and the relation between the marginal product of capital and the stock of, $mpc(k)$.

As Fig. 4.4 (a) shows, the eIES increases monotonically and converges asymptotically to a constant given by θ^{-1}. The present model implies a rising eIES during the transition period due to the technological possibilities of increasing the efficiency of labour by productive consumption. In contrast to the human-capital model discussed in the previous section, the eIES varies significantly. This indicates that the variation of the partial elasticity of the marginal NCC with respect to consumption, $\varepsilon(k,c)$, is comparably large: in the present case it ranges from -30 to 0. As has been noted in Section 4.3.1.4, several authors have reported empirical evidence in favour of a positive relation between the IES and per capita income (e.g. Ogaki, Ostry, and Reinhart, 1996). In addition, the model is consistent with diverging growth experiences in the presence of international capital markets because of the variable eIES (Rebelo, 1992).

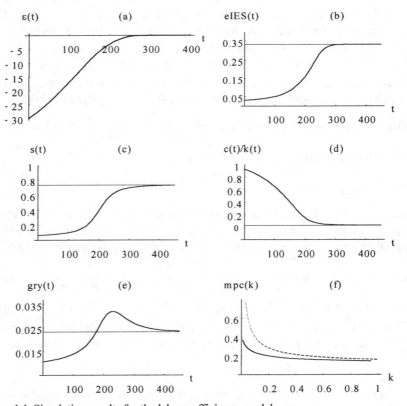

Fig. 4.4. Simulation results for the labour-efficiency model

Similar to the human-capital model discussed in the previous section, the saving rate increases monotonically during the transition and converges asymptotically towards its balanced-growth-equilibrium value [Fig. 4.4 (c)]. The possibility of productive consumption reduces the marginal NCC. As a result, a bias against saving occurs, which is especially marked for low per capita incomes and vanishes as per capita income grows without bound. In contrast to the human-capital model, the time path of the saving rate now appears mixed concave-convex, i.e. the saving rate increases only slightly at the beginning of the transition period.

Fig. 4.4 (f) shows the relation between the marginal product of capital and the stock of capital for the labour-efficiency model (solid line) and for the original Jones-Manuelli model with the production function: $y = B^{1-\alpha}k^{\alpha} + Gk$ (dashed line). It is a well-known quantitative problem of most versions of the neoclassical growth model that they imply extraordinarily high values of the marginal product of capital (King and Rebelo, 1993). The model under study implies significantly lower values of the marginal product of capital as illustrated by Fig. 4.4 (f). This effect is especially marked for low values of k. The economic reason is simply that capital is combined with less labour in units of efficiency compared to the original Jones-Manuelli model because the efficiency of labour is determined endogenously by the level of consumption.[157]

Fig. 4.4 (e) illustrates the possibility of non-monotonic dynamics of the growth rate of income. Specifically, the hump-shaped pattern of this time path implies a hump-shaped relation between the growth rate and the level of per capita income. Growth initially accelerates, reaches a maximum and subsequently decelerates. Therefore, the model enables an explanation of (conditional) ß-divergence for the lower range of income and (conditional) ß-convergence for the higher range of income.[158] Intuitively, this hump-shaped pattern of growth is the result of two opposing forces: First, productive consumption causes the saving rate to increase significantly during the transition to the BGP^{∞}. As a result, the growth rate of income rises as well. In addition, this mechanism is supported by the fact that the decrease in the marginal product of capital is not as strong as it is for the Jones-Manuelli model without productive consumption during early stages of economic development. Second, the marginal and average product of capital falls because of the neoclassical part of the production function, which causes the growth rate of income to decrease as well. In the present

---

[157] See Lucas (1990) for an alternative and complementary explanation of the comparably small international differences in the rate of returns observed in the real world, which relies on externalities of the average stock of human capital.

[158] This hump-shaped pattern of growth can be considered as representing a well-documented empirical regularity (e.g. Dollar, 1992 and Cho, 1994).

case, the first mechanism seems to dominate the second mechanism during early stages of economic development, while the reverse is true for later stages of economic development.

Finally, the rate of convergence to the asymptotic balanced-growth equilibrium seems to be remarkably small. The average rate of convergence calculated on the basis of the c/k-ratio for the first 100 years approximately amounts to 0.3 per cent. The simulation of the labour-efficiency model implies half-life times of about 150 years [Fig. 4.4(d)]. Accordingly, the persistence of diverse growth experiences, observable in the real world, can be basically explained to represent extraordinarily long transition processes to a unique balanced-growth equilibrium.

4.3.2.4 Summary and conclusion

Productive consumption was interpreted as increasing the efficiency of labour. The implications of this hypothesis for the intertemporal consumption trade-off and the process of growth were investigated within the labour-efficiency model. This model bears several interesting implications:

(1) Similar to the human-capital model, the harsh intertemporal consumption trade-off is modified. Along the optimal consumption path, the change of the marginal net cost of consumption (NCC) due to an increase in consumption as well as the change of the marginal NCC due to an increase in capital must be taken into account.

(2) The effective intertemporal elasticity of substitution (eIES) increases in the course of economic development because the partial elasticity of the marginal NCC with respect to consumption decreases. In contrast to the human-capital model, the simulation shows a considerable variation in the partial elasticity of the marginal NCC and hence a considerable variation in the eIES. The saving rate increases as well and shows a mixed convex-concave shape.

(3) The model under study implies significantly lower values of the marginal product of capital compared to the neoclassical growth model. This effect is especially marked for low values of capital per capita. The economic reason is simply that capital is combined with less labour in units of efficiency compared to a conventional set-up because the efficiency of labour is determined endogenously by the level of consumption.

(4) The simulation shows that the labour-efficiency model is able to reproduce the hump-shaped pattern of growth. Growth accelerates initially, reaches a maximum and decelerates subsequently. Therefore, the model enables an explanation of (conditional) ß-divergence for the lower range of per capita income and (conditional) ß-convergence for the higher range of per capita income.

4.4 Appendix

4.4.1 The human-capital model

Appendix 4-1: Human-capital-enhancement functions with constant η

The elasticity of the marginal NCC is defined as follows:

$$\eta(c) \equiv -\frac{c\psi''(c)}{\psi'(c)} = \frac{c\phi''(c)}{1-\phi'(c)}. \tag{A.4.1}$$

The class of human-capital-enhancement functions which imply a constant elasticity of the marginal NCC is derived as follows:

$$\frac{d}{dc}\ln[1-\phi'(c)] = -\frac{\eta}{c} \tag{A.4.2}$$

$$\ln[1-\phi'(c)] = -\eta\ln(c) + a_0 \tag{A.4.3}$$

$$1-\phi'(c) = c^{-\eta}e^{a_0} \tag{A.4.4}$$

$$\phi(c) = c - \frac{a_1}{1-\eta}c^{1-\eta} + a_2 \qquad \text{with} \quad a_1 \equiv e^{a_0}. \tag{A.4.5}$$

Appendix 4-2: Asymptotic saving rate

The gross saving rate as traditionally defined reads:

$$s \equiv \frac{\dot{k}_p + (\delta + n)k_p}{f(k)} = \frac{\dot{k} + (\delta + n)k - \phi(c)}{f(k)} = \frac{1}{f'(k)}\left[\frac{\dot{k}}{k} + (\delta + n) - \frac{\phi(c)}{k}\right]. \tag{A.4.6}$$

The first equality follows from (4.19) together with (4.22). From the properties of the human-capital-enhancement function and L'Hôpital's rule it follows that $\phi(c)/k$ vanishes asymptotically:

$$\lim_{t\to\infty}\frac{\phi[c(t)]}{k(t)} \leq \lim_{t\to\infty}\frac{\phi[f(k(t))]}{k(t)} = \lim_{t\to\infty}\frac{\phi'[f(k)]f'(k)\dot{k}(t)}{\dot{k}(t)} = 0. \tag{A.4.7}$$

Both $\phi[c(t)]$ and $k(t)$ must be positive and hence (A.4.7) implies that their ratio vanishes as time approaches infinity. Equation (4.40) shows that the common growth rate of c and k converges towards a constant asymptotically. From the set of equations (A.0.6), (A.4.7), and (4.40) it follows that the limit of the saving rate for $t \to \infty$ reads as follows (Barro and Sala-i-Martin, 1995, pp. 142/143):

$$\lim_{t \to \infty} s = \frac{1}{f'(k)}(\gamma_k * + \delta + n) = \frac{1}{f'(k)}\left[\frac{1}{\sigma}(f'(k) - \delta - \rho) + \delta + n\right]$$

$$= \frac{f'(k) - \rho + \sigma n + (\sigma - 1)\delta}{\sigma f'(k)}. \qquad (A.4.8)$$

The asymptotic balanced-growth saving rate of the linear growth model with productive consumption is constant and equals the saving rate of the underlying linear growth model.

Appendix 4-3: Stability of the asymptotic balanced-growth equilibrium

The proof of (local) stability of the asymptotic balanced-growth equilibrium comprises two steps (Koch, 1999): (i) The asymptotic direction of the BGP^∞ is determined and (ii) the asymptotic eigenvalues of the Jacobian matrix of the differential equation system along this direction are calculated.

In order to determine the direction of the BGP^∞, it is assumed that $c = Dk$ for some unknown D, i.e. $\displaystyle\lim_{k \to \infty} \frac{\dot{c}(Dk)}{k(k,Dk)} = D$ has to be solved for D:

$$\lim_{k \to \infty} \frac{Dk[f'(k) - \delta - \rho]/[\sigma - \eta(Dk)]}{[f'(k) - \delta - n]k - \psi(Dk)} = D. \qquad (A.4.9)$$

Applying L'Hôpital's rule yields:

$$\lim_{k \to \infty} \frac{\left\{\left[D(f'(k) - \delta - \rho) + Dk\overbrace{f''(k)}^{=0}\right] \cdot [\sigma - \eta(Dk)] - \atop Dk[f'(k) - \delta - \rho] \cdot [-D\eta'(Dk)]\right\} \cdot [\sigma - \eta(Dk)]^{-2}}{f'(k) - \delta - n - D\psi'(Dk)} = D.$$

$$(A.\,4.10)$$

Provided that the limit of $k\eta'(Dk) = D^{-1}c\eta'(c)$ for $k \to \infty$ is zero and bearing in mind that $\displaystyle\lim_{k \to \infty}\eta(Dk) = \eta'(Dk) = 0$ and $\displaystyle\lim_{k \to \infty}\psi'(Dk) = 1$, equation (A. 4.10) reduces to:

$$\frac{D[f'(k)-\delta-\rho]/\sigma}{f'(k)-\delta-n-D}=D.$$

(A.4.11)

The requirement that $\lim_{c\to\infty} c\eta'(c)=0$ is met for the following specific human-capital-enhancement functions: $\phi(c)=c^{\beta}$ with $0<\beta<1$ and $\phi(c)=Bc/(B+c)$, where B denotes a positive constant. Equation (A.4.11) possesses two solutions: $D_1=0$ and

$D_2=f'(k)-\delta-n-\sigma^{-1}[f'(k)-\delta-\rho]$. The trajectory associated with the asymptotic direction $D_1=0$ violates the transversality condition and thus has to be excluded.[159] The latter solution, D_2, shows the (asymptotic) direction of the BGP^{∞} which equals the direction of the BGP of the underlying linear growth model (e.g. Barro and Sala-i-Martin, 1995, p. 143).

In the next step, the Jacobian matrix of the underlying differential equation system is calculated and the limit of its eigenvalues is taken for $c=Dk$ and $k\to\infty$. The Jacobian of (4.35) and the equation of motion of k stated in (4.23) reads as follows:

$$\mathbf{J}=\begin{pmatrix} \dfrac{[f'(k)-\delta-\rho]/\sigma-[f'(k)-\delta-\rho]\eta(c)-c[f'(k)-\delta-\rho]\cdot[-\eta'(c)]}{[\sigma-\eta(c)]^2} & 0 \\ -\psi'(c) & f'(k)-\delta-n \end{pmatrix}.$$

(A.4.12)

The eigenvalues (or characteristic roots) of $\mathbf{J}$ are the solutions to $|\mathbf{J}-\lambda\mathbf{I}|=0$:

$$\left\{\frac{[f'(k)-\delta-\rho]/\sigma-[f'(k)-\delta-\rho]\eta(c)-c[f'(k)-\delta-\rho]\cdot[-\eta'(c)]}{[\sigma-\eta(c)]^2}-\lambda\right\}\times$$
$$[f'(k)-\delta-n-\lambda]=0.$$

(A.4.13)

---

[159] By considering the dynamic efficiency condition (4.27) for interior solutions, the transversality condition can be written as $\lim_{t\to\infty} e^{[\delta+n-f'(k)]\cdot t}\lambda(0)k(t)=0$. With respect to the equation of motion of k stated in (4.23), the asymptotic growth rate of k in the case of $\gamma_c<\gamma_k$ is $f'(k)-\delta-n$. Consequently, the transversality condition would be violated.

Provided that $c\eta'(c)$ converges to zero as c approaches infinity the limit of the eigenvalues for $c = Dk$ and $k \to \infty$ are the solution to:

$$[(f'(k)-\delta-\rho)\sigma^{-1}-\lambda]\cdot[f'(k)-\delta-n-\lambda]=0,\qquad(A.4.14)$$

which implies that $\lambda_1 = \sigma^{-1}[f'(k)-\delta-\rho]$ and $\lambda_2 = f'(k)-\delta-n$. Both eigenvalues are positive.[160] λ_1 is the asymptotic balanced growth rate. Therefore, $\lambda_2 > 0$ implies that the BGP^∞ with asymptotic slope $D > 0$ is saddle-point stable and all other trajectory diverge, i.e. the optimal solution is unique (Koch, 1999, Theorem 3.1).

4.4.2 The labour-efficiency model

Appendix 4-4: Derivation of the modified Keynes-Ramsey rule

The dynamic optimisation problem for the labour-efficiency model reads:

$$\max_{\{c(t)\}} \int_0^\infty u[c(t)]\cdot e^{-(\rho-n)\cdot t}\,dt$$

s.t. $\quad \dot{k}(t) = f[k(t),c(t)]-(\delta+n)k(t)-c(t)$

$\qquad k(0)=k_0 \quad k(t)\geq0$

$\qquad 0\leq c(t)\leq f[k(t),c(t)],\qquad(A.4.15)$

and the current-value Hamiltonian accordingly is (time index omitted):

$$H(c,k,\lambda)=u(c)+\lambda[f(k,c)-(\delta+n)k-c].\qquad(A.4.16)$$

Application of the maximum principle leads to the necessary first-order conditions for interior solutions:[161]

---

[160] Unbounded growth requires $\sigma^{-1}[f'(k)-\delta-\rho]>0$. The finiteness of the utility integral requires that $f'(k)-\delta-n-\sigma^{-1}[f'(k)-\delta-\rho]>0$ (e.g. Barro and Sala-i-Martin, 1995, pp. 142/143) and hence $f'(k)-\delta-n>0$.

[161] Because the Hamiltonian is concave in the control and the state, the necessary conditions are also sufficient for a maximum. In addition to the first-order conditions, an optimal trajectory must satisfy the transversality condition: $\lim_{t\to\infty} e^{-(\rho-n)\cdot t}\lambda(t)k(t)=0$.

$$\frac{\partial H}{\partial \lambda} = \dot{k} = f(k,c) - (\delta + n)k - c \tag{A.4.17}$$

$$\dot{\lambda} = \lambda(\rho - n) - \frac{\partial H}{\partial k} = \lambda \left[\rho + \delta - \frac{\partial f(k,c)}{\partial k} \right] \tag{A.4.18}$$

$$\frac{\partial H}{\partial c} = u'(c) + \lambda \left[\frac{\partial f(k,c)}{\partial c} - 1 \right] = 0. \tag{A.4.19}$$

Differentiation of (A.4.19) with respect to time gives:

$$u''(c)\dot{c} = \dot{\lambda} \left[1 - \frac{\partial f(k,c)}{\partial c} \right] + \lambda \left[-\dot{c} \frac{\partial^2 f(k,c)}{\partial c^2} - \dot{k} \frac{\partial^2 f(k,c)}{\partial c \partial k} \right] \tag{A.4.20}$$

and subsequently dividing by the original relation (A.4.19) yields:

$$\frac{u''(c)\dot{c}}{u'(c)} = \frac{\dot{\lambda}}{\lambda} + \frac{-\dot{c} \dfrac{\partial^2 f(k,c)}{\partial c^2}}{1 - \dfrac{\partial f(k,c)}{\partial c}} + \frac{-\dot{k} \dfrac{\partial^2 f(k,c)}{\partial c \partial k}}{1 - \dfrac{\partial f(k,c)}{\partial c}}. \tag{A.4.21}$$

Using (A.4.18) for eliminating the shadow price and noting the definition of the IES, the preceding equation can be written as:

$$\frac{\dot{c}}{c} = [\sigma - \varepsilon(k,c)]^{-1} \cdot \left[\frac{\partial f(k,c)}{\partial k} - \delta - \rho + \frac{\dot{k}}{k} \gamma(k,c) \right]$$

with

$$\varepsilon(k,c) \equiv -\frac{\dfrac{\partial \varphi(k,c)}{\partial c} c}{\varphi(k,c)} = \frac{\dfrac{\partial^2 f(k,c)}{\partial c^2} c}{1 - \dfrac{\partial f(k,c)}{\partial c}} < 0$$

$$\gamma(k,c) \equiv -\frac{\dfrac{\partial \varphi(k,c)}{\partial k} k}{\varphi(k,c)} = \frac{\dfrac{\partial^2 f(k,c)}{\partial c \partial k} k}{1 - \dfrac{\partial f(k,c)}{\partial c}} > 0, \tag{A.4.22}$$

which is the modified Keynes-Ramsey rule of the labour-efficiency model [equation (4.42) in the text].

Appendix 4-5: Stability of the asymptotic balanced-growth equilibrium

In order to determine the asymptotic direction of the BGP^∞, it is assumed that $c = Dk$ for some unknown D, i.e. $\lim\limits_{k \to \infty} \dfrac{\dot{c}(k,Dk)}{\dot{k}(k,Dk)} = D$ has to be solved for D:

$$\lim_{k \to \infty} \frac{Dk[\sigma - \varepsilon(k,Dk)]^{-1}\left[\dfrac{\partial f(k,Dk)}{\partial k} - \delta - \rho + \gamma(k,Dk)\cdot\left(\dfrac{f(k,Dk)}{k} - (\delta + n) - D\right)\right]}{f(k,Dk) - (\delta + n)k - Dk} = D$$

(A.4.23)

Provided that $\varepsilon(k,Dk)$ and $\gamma(k,Dk)$ vanish for $k \to \infty$, equation (A.4.23) can be written as follows:

$$\frac{D(G - \delta - \rho)\sigma^{-1}}{G - \delta - n - D} = D,$$

(A.4.24)

where $G > 0$ denotes the limit of the average and marginal product of capital for $k \to \infty$. The preceding equation has two solutions: $D_1 = 0$ and $D_2 = G - \delta - n - \sigma^{-1}(G - \delta - \rho)$. The trajectory associated with the asymptotic direction $D_1 = 0$ violates the transversality condition and hence has to be excluded.[162] The latter solution shows the (asymptotic) direction of the BGP^∞ which equals the direction of the BGP of the underlying linear growth model (e.g. Barro and Sala-i-Martin, 1995, p. 143).

The preceding argumentation requires that both $\varepsilon(k,c)$ and $\gamma(k,c)$ vanish for $c = Dk$ and $k \to \infty$. In what follows, the validity of this assumption is demonstrated concisely in the case of the specific production function with endogenous efficiency of labour: $f(k,c) = A(c)^{1-\alpha}k^\alpha + Gk$.

---

[162] The dynamic efficiency condition (A.4.18) indicates that the asymptotic growth rate of the term $e^{-(\rho-n)\cdot t}\lambda(t)$ reads $\delta + n - f_k(k,c)$. With respect to (A.4.15), the asymptotic growth rate of k in the case of $\gamma_c < \gamma_k$ reads $f(k,c)k^{-1} - \delta - n$. Provided that $\lim\limits_{t \to \infty} f(k,c)k^{-1} = \lim\limits_{t \to \infty} f_k(k,c)$, the transversality condition, stated in footnote 154, would be violated (e.g. Barro and Sala-i-Martin, 1995, p. 65).

On this occasion, two specific labour-efficiency functions are considered: $A(c) = c^\beta$ and $A(c) = Bc/(B+c)$.

In the case of the first specific labour-efficiency function, the production function reads: $f(k,c) = c^{\beta(1-\alpha)} k^\alpha + Gk$. The derivatives which occur in $\varepsilon(k,c)$ and $\gamma(k,c)$ are as follows:[163] $f_c(k,c) = \beta(1-\alpha)c^{\beta(1-\alpha)-1} k^\alpha$, $f_{cc}(k,c) = \beta(1-\alpha)[\beta(1-\alpha)-1]c^{\beta(1-\alpha)-2} k^\alpha$, and $f_{ck}(k,c) = \alpha\beta(1-\alpha)c^{\beta(1-\alpha)-1} k^{\alpha-1}$. The elasticities under consideration can be written as $\varepsilon(k,c) \equiv \dfrac{f_{cc}(k,c)c}{1 - f_c(k,c)}$ and $\gamma(k,c) \equiv \dfrac{f_{ck}(k,c)k}{1 - f_c(k,c)}$. Now, the limit of both elasticities evaluated along the constant direction of the BGP^∞, i.e. for $c = Dk$ and for $k \to \infty$, is considered. As a result of the parameter restriction $0 < \beta < 1$, the denominator of both elasticities converges to unity for $k \to \infty$ because $\beta(1-\alpha)-1+\alpha < 0$. The same argument guarantees that the nominator of both elasticities vanishes asymptotically and hence both elasticities vanish for $k \to \infty$.

In the case of the second labour-efficiency function, the production function reads: $f(k,c) = [Bc/(B+c)]^{(1-\alpha)} k^\alpha + Gk$. The explicit calculation of $\varepsilon(k,c)$ and $\gamma(k,c)$ would yield very unwieldy expressions. Therefore, the elasticities are calculated and factored by means of Mathematica®. Fig. 4.5 shows the corresponding Mathematica® codes and evaluated output.

The expressions for $\varepsilon(k,c)$ and $\gamma(k,c)$ as shown in output row (6) and (7), vanish for $k \to \infty$ because the highest exponent of k is greater for the (expanded) denominator compared to the (expanded) nominator.

The second step of the proof of stability is carried out numerically employing the same specific functions and parameter values which have been used for the simulation. The reason for this procedure is that explicit calculation would yield untractable expressions. Fig. 4.6 shows the numerical computation of the eigenvalues of the Jacobian.

---

[163] $f_{x_i}(x_i)$ is used as a short-hand symbol for the first partial derivative of $f(x_i)$ with respect to the i-th argument, i.e. $f_{x_i}(x_i) \equiv \partial f(x_i)/\partial x_i$ and $f_{x_i x_i}(x_i) \equiv \partial^2 f(x_i)/\partial x_i^2$.

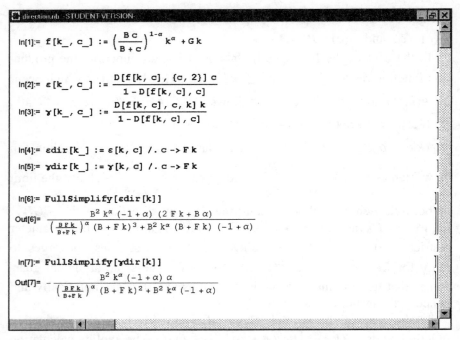

Fig. 4.5. Partial elasticities of the marginal net cost of consumption

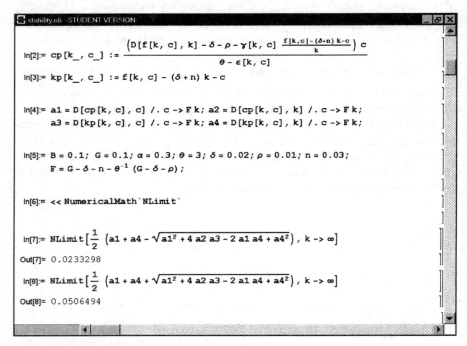

Fig. 4.6. Numerical determination of asymptotic eigenvalues

The limits of the eigenvalues of the Jacobian are evaluated for $c = Dk$ and $k \to \infty$. Both eigenvalues are positive, as shown in output row (7) and (8). The eigenvalue shown in output row (7) is approximately the balanced growh rate. Hence, the BGP^∞ with the asymptotic slope $D_2 > 0$ is saddle-point stable and all other trajectory diverge, i.e. the optimal solution is unique (Koch, 1999, Theorem 3.1).

5 Transitional dynamics with endogenous control variables[*]

5.1 Introduction

The issue of 'convergence' represents one of the big topics within current economic literature (Pritchett, 1996, p. 40). Initially, the question was simply whether poor countries are catching up with rich countries, i.e. whether there is convergence in per capita incomes. After having recognised that unconditional convergence is not taking place, the theoretical and empirical literature has centred around the conditional convergence hypothesis of the neoclassical growth model.

The discussion about convergence gave rise to a coherent framework which comprises theoretical concepts as well as empirical methods. The widely employed method of cross-sectional conditional convergence regression is crucially based on the concept of control variables, which are assumed to proxy the balanced-growth path. On account of the definition of the balanced-growth path, the control variables are usually considered as being constant in the course of economic development. However, there are strong theoretical arguments and solid empirical support for the view that at least a subset of the control variables, like the investment rates in physical and human capital and the rate of population growth, varies systematically with the level of per capita income. The explicit consideration of the possibility of endogenous control variables has two important consequences. The first is purely econometric and concerns the choice of the appropriate estimation procedure in order to obtain unbiased and consistent coefficient estimates. The second concerns the theoretical interpretation of the conditional convergence results. Accordingly, the variation of some of the control variables with the level and the growth rate of per capita income contains important information about the transition to the balanced-growth equilibrium rather than information about the balanced-growth equilibrium itself. In order to exploit this information the coefficients of the control variables from the conditional convergence regression are combined with the corresponding elasticities of the control variables with

---

[*]This chapter is based on Steger (2000c).

respect to per capita income. The resulting expression describes the change in the growth rate of per capita income caused by an increase in the level of per capita income while accounting for the endogenous variation of the control variables. In other words, this procedure enables the identification of several mechanisms of conditional ß-convergence and conditional ß-divergence.

This chapter is organised as follows: Section 5.2 offers a selective overview of the cross-sectional convergence debate, including a theoretical discussion of structural convergence equations, the main results of the empirical literature, and a discussion of some of the methodological issues. Section 5.3 contains a cross-sectional convergence analysis which focuses explicitly on the endogeneity of the control variables. The method employed allows to identify empirically several mechanisms of conditional ß-convergence and ß-divergence. Finally, Section 5.4 presents a summary and conclusion.

5.2 The convergence debate: a selective overview

5.2.1 Structural convergence equations

This section demonstrates concisely the derivation of structural convergence equations and discusses their main observable implications. The term 'structural convergence equation' denotes those convergence equations which are derived from an explicit growth model (de la Fuente, 1997, p. 52). Subsequently, the connection between structural convergence equations and convergence or growth regressions is illustrated.[164] For this purpose, consider at first the following ordinary autonomous differential equation $\dot{x}(t) = F[x(t)]$, which is assumed to possess an equilibrium defined by $F(x^*) = 0$. In the neighbourhood of this stationary point the *rate* or *speed of convergence* of $x(t)$ can be determined by means of a first-order Taylor approximation around x^* (e.g. Romer, 1996, pp. 21-23):

$$\dot{x}(t) \cong F(x^*) + F'(x^*) \cdot [x(t) - x^*]. \tag{5.1}$$

By noting that by definition $F(x^*) = 0$, the previous equation can be written as follows:

$$\dot{x}(t) \cong -\lambda[x(t) - x^*] \quad \text{with} \quad \lambda \equiv -F'(x^*). \tag{5.2}$$

---

[164] The expressions 'convergence regressions' and 'growth regressions' are used as synonyms in the literature (Temple, 1999, pp. 11 and 16); however the term growth regressions should not be confused with growth accounting regressions (Temple, 1999, p. 17).

The coefficient λ, as defined by (5.2), describes the (instantaneous) rate of convergence.[165] As a result of the linearisation of the original differential equation, the variable $x(t)$ converges at a constant rate to its equilibrium value. Equation (5.2) can be considered as a (linear) differential equation in the variable $z(t) \equiv x(t) - x^*$ with the following solution: $z(t) = z(0) \cdot e^{-\lambda t}$. This equation leads to another frequently used definition of the rate of convergence (e.g. Romer, 1996, p. 22):

$$\lambda \equiv -\ln\left(\frac{x(t) - x^*}{x(0) - x^*}\right) / t. \tag{5.3}$$

It should be noted that (5.3) describes the average rate of convergence over the time interval $[0,t]$, which is identical to the instantaneous rate of convergence as shown in (5.2) only if the underlying differential equation is linear. The limit of both definitions of the rate of convergence given by (5.2) and (5.3) for $t \to \infty$ is identical. In addition, the definition (5.3) immediately leads to the relation between the (average) rate of convergence and the half-life time, denoted as $t_{0.5}$, which accordingly reads: $t_{0.5} = -\ln(0.5)/\lambda$.

Because the theoretical and empirical literature is almost exclusively based on logarithmic variables, it is worth noting that the preceding result equally holds for the logarithm of $x(t)$.[166] In order to demonstrate this point consider the following ordinary autonomous differential equation in the logarithm of $x(t)$, i.e. $\dfrac{d}{dt}\ln[x(t)] = F\{\ln[x(t)]\}$ which can be equivalently expressed as follows:

$$\frac{d}{dt}\ln[x(t)] = x(t)^{-1}\dot{x}(t) = e^{-\ln[x(t)]}F[e^{\ln[x(t)]}] \equiv G\{\ln[x(t)]\}. \tag{5.4}$$

Carrying out the same steps as before yields:

$$\frac{d}{dt}\ln[\dot{x}(t)] \cong \underbrace{G\{\ln[x(t)^*]\}}_{=0} + G'[\ln(x^*)] \cdot \{\ln[x(t)] - \ln(x^*)\}. \tag{5.5}$$

By noting that

---

[165] This definition has already been used in Section 3.3; see equation (3.18).
[166] The possibility to formulate the structural convergence equation as an additive combination of economic variables expressed in more or less observable units might explain that logarithmic variables are widely used; see equation (5.16).

$$G'[\ln(x^*)] = -e^{-\ln(x^*)} \underbrace{F[e^{\ln(x^*)}]}_{=0} + e^{-\ln(x^*)} e^{\ln(x^*)} F'(e^{\ln(x^*)}) = F'(e^{\ln(x^*)}),$$

(5.6)

equation (5.5) can be written as follows:

$$\frac{d}{dt}\ln[x(t)] \cong F'[e^{\ln(x^*)}] \cdot \{\ln[x(t)] - \ln(x^*)\}.$$

(5.7)

Moreover, the preceding equation can be equally expressed as

$$\frac{d}{dt}\ln[x(t)] \cong -\lambda\{\ln[x(t)] - \ln(x^*)\}$$

with $\lambda \equiv -F'[e^{\ln(x^*)}] = -F'(x^*).$

(5.8)

Comparing (5.8) with (5.2) it becomes evident that locally around the equilibrium the logarithm of $x(t)$ converges at the same rate as $x(t)$ itself.

The structural convergence equation is usually derived from the neoclassical model of growth. Consequently, the differential equation in the stock of capital per effective units of labour, which describes the dynamics of the neoclassical model with exogenous saving and (exogenous) technical progress, is the natural starting point:[167]

$$\hat{k}(t) = s f[\hat{k}(t)] - (n + \delta + x)\hat{k}(t),$$

(5.9)

where s denotes the constant saving rate, $f(\hat{k})$ a neoclassical production function, $\hat{k}$ the stock of capital per effective units of labour, n the growth rate of labour, δ the depreciation rate of capital, and x the rate of technical progress, respectively.[168] Provided that the Inada conditions hold $[f'(\hat{k}) > 0, \quad f''(\hat{k}) < 0, \quad \lim_{t \to 0} f'(\hat{k}) = \infty, \quad \lim_{t \to \infty} f'(\hat{k}) = 0]$ and $n + \delta + x > 0$, this non-linear differential equation in $\hat{k}$ possesses at least one equilibrium. This equilibrium is denoted by $\hat{k}*$ and is implicitly de-

---

[167] The convergence implication of the neoclassical growth model and its alleged incompatibility with the data was an empirical motivation for endogenous growth theory. Specifically, the absence of unconditional ß-convergence was regarded as evidence against the neoclassical model and in favour of endogenous growth models. However, at least two qualifications are necessary at this point: (i) the neoclassical model implies conditional as opposed to unconditional ß-convergence (e.g. Barro and Sala-i-Martin, 1992) and (ii) even endogenous growth models are compatible with (conditional) ß-convergence (Sala-i-Martin, 1996b, p. 1035). The empirical discrimination between neoclassical and endogenous growth models is still an open research topic (Kocherlakota and Yi, 1995 and Sala-i-Martin, 1996a, p. 1345, fn. 12).

[168] In order to simplify the notation, the time index is omitted.

fined by $sf(\hat{k}^*) = (n + \delta + x)\hat{k}^*$. According to (5.2) the rate of convergence of capital per effective units of labour reads: $\lambda = -[sf'(\hat{k}^*) - (n + \delta + x)]$. Substituting $(n + \delta + x)\hat{k}^* / f(\hat{k}^*)$ for s and bearing in mind the definition of the partial elasticity of output with respect to capital evaluated at equilibrium, $\alpha(\hat{k}^*) \equiv f'(\hat{k}^*)\hat{k}^* / f(\hat{k}^*)$, the analogue of equation (5.2) for the variable $\hat{k}$ can be written as follows:

$$\dot{\hat{k}} \cong -\lambda(\hat{k} - \hat{k}^*) \text{ with } \quad \lambda \equiv [1 - \alpha(\hat{k}^*)] \cdot (n + \delta + x) > 0 . \tag{5.10}$$

The same is true if the logarithm of capital per effective labour is used:

$$\frac{d}{dt}\ln(\hat{k}) \cong -\lambda[\ln(\hat{k}) - \ln(\hat{k}^*)]$$

with $\quad \lambda \equiv [1 - \alpha(\hat{k}^*)] \cdot (n + \delta + x) > 0 .$ \hfill (5.11)

The solution to this linear differential equation is given by:

$$\ln[\hat{k}(t)] - \ln(\hat{k}^*) \cong [\ln[\hat{k}(0)] - \ln(\hat{k}^*)]e^{-\lambda t} . \tag{5.12}$$

It can be shown that locally around the dynamic equilibrium income per effective units of labour, $\hat{y} = f(\hat{k})$, approaches $\hat{y}^*$ at the same rate as $\hat{k}$ approaches $\hat{k}^*$ (Romer, 1996, p. 22 and Durlauf and Quah, 1998, p. 16):[169]

$$\ln[\hat{y}(t)] - \ln(\hat{y}^*) \cong [\ln[\hat{y}(0)] - \ln(\hat{y}^*)]e^{-\lambda t} \tag{5.13}$$

With regard to an empirical examination of the convergence implication, it is important to notice that neither (5.12) nor (5.13) in conjunction with (5.11) represent empirically refutable hypotheses. The reason simply is that the variables $\hat{k}(t)$ or $\hat{y}(t)$ are not observable. Merely per capita income as opposed to income per effective units of labour can be observed in the real world. Therefore, it is necessary to express equation (5.13) in variables which can be observed. By recalling that $y(t) = \hat{y}(t)A(t)$, equation (5.13) can be expressed as follows (Durlauf and Quah, 1998, p. 18):

$$\ln[y(t)] = \ln[A(0)] + xt + \ln[\hat{y}^*] + \{\ln[y(0)] - [\ln[\hat{y}^*] + \ln[A(0)]]\}e^{-\lambda t} . \tag{5.14}$$

---

[169] A relation equivalent to equation (5.13) can be derived from the necessary first-order conditions emerging within the frame of the Ramsey-Cass-Koopmans model (Barro and Sala-i-Martin, 1992, p. 225; Barro and Sala-i-Martin, 1995, Appendix 2A; and Durlauf and Quah, 1998, pp. 12-17). In this case the rate of convergence is a more complicated function of preference and technology parameters.

Equation (5.14) illustrates that the time path of per capita income contains two components: First, the levels component completely describes the level and the slope of the balanced-growth path and comprises the first three terms on the right-hand side of (5.14). Second, the convergence component describes the deviation of per capita income from its balanced-growth equilibrium. This second component is represented by the last term on the right-hand side of (5.14) and vanishes at the constant rate λ, the rate of convergence. The levels component reflects balanced-growth dynamics while the convergence component reflects transitional dynamics (Durlauf and Quah, 1998, p. 18).[170]

Fig. 5.1 shows the different possible qualitative convergence implications of the neoclassical model. Fig. 5.1 (a) illustrates *absolute* or *unconditional ß-convergence*: In the absence of shocks poor economies grow faster than rich economies, i.e. the slope of the time path $\ln[y(t)]$ is greater for poor countries compared to rich countries. This concept of unconditional ß-convergence implicitly supposes that all economies converge to the same balanced-growth path. Stated differently, the unconditional convergence hypothesis supposes that international symmetry with respect to preferences and technology applies (Rebelo, 1992, p. 7). If it is, on the other hand, admitted that economies differ with respect to preferences and technology (as well as some political variables), the concept of *conditional ß-convergence* turns out to be appropriate. Accordingly, Fig. 5.1 (b) shows two time paths of per capita income which converge to different balanced-growth equilibria. In this case, the neoclassical model merely implies that the growth rate of per capita income is inversely related to the distance between the current level of per capita income and its balanced-growth equilibrium. As illustrated in Fig. 5.1 (b), the conditional convergence hypothesis is consistent with the observation that poor countries grow faster than rich countries.[171]

---

[170] It should be noted that (5.14) is the time path of per capita income valid within a 'small' neighbourhood of the balanced-growth equilibrium. However, Ortigueira and Santos (1997, pp. 390/391) demonstrate that the local rate of convergence around the dynamic equilibrium is a good estimate for the global convergence behaviour within a wide range of capital per capita in the case of the neoclassical model.

[171] The distinction between conditional and unconditional convergence was first introduced by Sala-i-Martin (1990) as Sala-i-Martin (1996b, p. 1020) notices. For a comprehensive discussion of the concept of ß-convergence as well as its relation to σ − convergence see Sala-i-Martin (1996b).

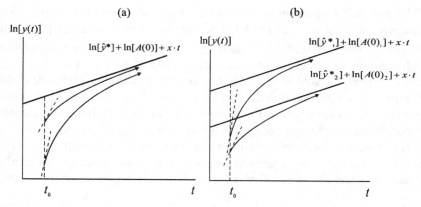

Fig. 5.1. Unconditional and conditional convergence
Source: Following Durlauf and Quah (1998, Figure 4).

In order to illustrate the quantitative convergence implication of the neoclassical model Barro and Sala-i-Martin (1995, pp. 37/38) use a set of benchmark parameter values with $x = 0.02$, $n = 0.01$, $\delta = 0.05$ (per year), and $\alpha = 0.33$. In this case the model implies a rate of convergence of approximately 0.056 per year which corresponds to a half-life time of 12.5 years. In summary, the (conditional) convergence hypothesis of the neoclassical growth model represents an empirically refutable hypothesis which contains a qualitative as well as a quantitative dimension.

From equation (5.14) the average growth rate of per capita income over some time interval $[0,t]$ can be expressed as follows:

$$\frac{\ln[y(t)] - \ln[y(0)]}{t} = x - \frac{(1 - e^{-\lambda t})}{t}\{\ln[y(0)] - [\ln[\hat{y}^*] + \ln[A(0)] + x0]\}.$$

(5.15)

The average growth rate of per capita income over the time interval $[0,t]$ equals the rate of technical progress plus a transition component; notice that the last term on the right-hand side is negative provided that the economy approaches its balanced-growth equilibrium from below. Equation (5.15) can be equivalently expressed as follows:

$$\gamma_{0,t} = x + \frac{1 - e^{-\lambda t}}{t}\{\ln[A(0)] + \ln[\hat{y}^*]\} - \frac{1 - e^{-\lambda t}}{t}\ln[y(0)]$$

with $\gamma_{0,t} \equiv \dfrac{\ln[y(t)] - \ln[y(0)]}{t}$.

(5.16)

The preceding equation is taken to be the main observable implication of the neoclassical growth model. For any fixed time interval $[0,t]$ the average growth rate additively consists of several constant components which contain information on balanced-growth dynamics [the first two terms on the right-hand side of (5.16)] and on transitional dynamics [the last term on the right-hand side of (5.16)]. Now, if a cross-section of countries over a fixed time interval is considered, equation (5.16) demonstrates that conditional ß-convergence ($\lambda > 0$) implies a negative partial correlation (i.e. holding the determinants of the balanced-growth path fixed) between the average annual growth rate and the initial level of per capita income. Expressed more formally, (5.16) immediately implies that

$$\frac{\partial \gamma_{0,t}}{\partial \ln[y(0)]} = -\frac{1-e^{-\lambda \cdot t}}{t} < 0 \text{ if } \lambda > 0.$$

The usual empirical cross-sectional growth regression stems directly from the theoretical convergence equation (5.16) and can be written as follows (e.g. Barro and Sala-i-Martin, 1992, p. 227; Mankiw, Romer, and Weil, 1992, p. 423; and Sala-i-Martin, 1996b, p. 1027):

$$\gamma_{i,0,t} = a_0 - a_1 \ln(y_{i,0}) + \mathbf{v}\mathbf{x}_i + \varepsilon_{i,0,t}, \tag{5.17}$$

where $\gamma_{i,0,t}$ denotes the average annual growth rate of per capita income over the period $[0,t]$ for country i, a_0 a positive constant, $y_{i,0}$ the initial level of per capita income, $\mathbf{v}$ a vector of further regression coefficients, $\mathbf{x}_i$ a vector of so-called control variables and $\varepsilon_{i,0,t}$ an independently and identically distributed error term with mean zero, respectively. The variables in $\mathbf{x}$ are supposed to capture the determinants of the balanced-growth path. A vast empirical literature has identified about 50 variables which are correlated with the (average) growth rate of per capita income (e.g. Kormendi and Meguire, 1985; Barro, 1991; and Barro and Sala-i-Martin, 1995, pp. 422-424 and 436-444).[172] The list of control variables includes, among others, the investment rates for physical and human capital (e.g. school enrolment ratios), the share of government consumption in GDP, the black-market premium, as well as measures of political instability (e.g. Klenow and Rodríguez-Clare, 1997, pp. 599/600).[173] By controlling for those variables which determine the balanced-growth path, the convergence coefficient [a_1 in equation (5.17)] shows the partial

---

[172] Durlauf and Quah (1998, Table 5.2) present a very comprehensive overview of the literature.

[173] However, Levine and Renelt (1992) argue that only a small number of variables are robustly correlated with the growth rate of per capita income.

correlation between the average growth rate and the initial level of per capita income. The rate of conditional ß-convergence can be deduced from the estimate of this convergence coefficient by remembering that:

$$\frac{\partial \gamma_{i,0,t}}{\partial \ln(y_{i,0})} = -a_1 = -\frac{1-e^{-\lambda \cdot t}}{t}. \tag{5.18}$$

A positive *convergence coefficient* ($a_1 > 0$) according to (5.18) immediately implies a positive value for the *rate of convergence* ($\lambda > 0$) indicating (conditional) ß-convergence.[174] On the other hand, a negative convergence coefficient ($a_1 < 0$) in the same way implies a negative value of the rate of convergence ($\lambda < 0$) indicating (conditional) ß-divergence. The relation between the convergence coefficient and the rate of convergence can be further illustrated by solving (5.18) for the rate of convergence which yields: $\lambda = -\ln(1-a_1 t)/t$. Fig. 5.2 shows the rate of convergence as a function of the convergence coefficient for $t = 25$.

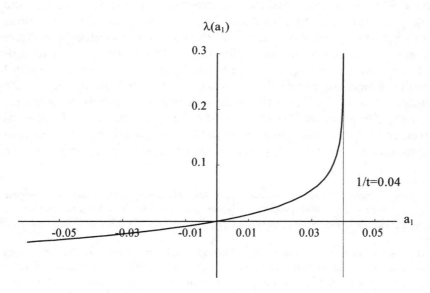

Fig. 5.2. Relation between the rate of convergence and the convergence coefficient

---

[174] In order to avoid any confusion, the terminological distinction between the convergence coefficient, which can be estimated empirically, and the rate of convergence, which is implied by the numerical value of the convergence coefficient according to (5.18), should be recognised.

The rate of convergence, $\lambda(a_1)$, is negative for negative values of the convergence coefficient, a_1, and *vice versa*. The rate of convergence approaches infinity as a_1 converges to $1/t$ and is not defined for $a_1 > 1/t$. In addition, Fig. 5.2 illustrates that the rate of convergence depends very sensitively on the estimated convergence coefficient; notice that the scaling of the vertical and the horizontal axes differ.

5.2.2 Main empirical results

Baumol (1986) was the first to estimate convergence regressions. Using long-run data from Maddison (1979), he analysed the growth experiences of sixteen industrialised countries by estimating an *unconditional convergence equation*.[175] He estimated a value of -0.75 for the convergence coefficient, which shows the correlation between the average annual growth rate of GDP per work hour (1870-1979) and the logarithm of GDP per work hour in 1979 (Baumol, 1986, p. 1076). This result implies ß-convergence for the group of countries under study.[176] [177] However, De Long (1988) argues that Baumol's convergence outcome is largely the result of an *ex-post* sample selection bias. The sample in question is made up of *ex-post* successful countries and the convergence outcome is therefore almost guaranteed automatically. Barro (1991) was the first to estimate *conditional convergence regressions* by employing a set of control variables which are expected to capture international differences in the balanced-growth path.[178] On the basis of a broad sample of 98 countries [1960-85, Summers and Heston (1988) data], he finds conditional ß-convergence. After controlling for initial human capital, government consumption, public investment, political stability, and market distortions, the

---

[175] Although Baumol (1986) estimates an unconditional convergence equation, the analysis could be interpreted as conditional convergence analysis. The reason simply is that the underlying sample represents a relatively homogenous group of economies (Sala-i-Martin, 1996b).

[176] There seems to be a 'sign confusion' within the empirical convergence literature: With respect to the structural convergence equation (5.16), the convergence regression should be of the form $\gamma = x - a\ln[y(0)] + e$ and ß-convergence would require $a > 0$ (Sala-i-Martin, 1996b, p. 1042). However, other authors specify the growth regression in the form $\gamma = x + a\ln[y(0)] + e$ and in this case $a < 0$ indicates ß-convergence (Mankiw, Romer, and Weil, 1992, p. 425).

[177] Moreover, on the basis of the comprehensive Summers and Heston data set, Baumol (1986, pp. 1079-1081) argues that there are three separate convergence clubs.

[178] For this reason, conditional convergence regressions are sometimes labelled as 'Barro regressions'. In the cross-sectional convergence literature, more than 50 control variables have been used within this framework of analysis; see Durlauf and Quah (1998, Table 2) for a very comprehensive survey of this literature.

conditional convergence coefficient is estimated to be -0.074 (Barro, 1991, Table 1, pp. 410-413).

Barro and Sala-i-Martin (1992) estimate a version of the convergence equation (5.16) for 47 US states (1880-1988) and report a rate of convergence of 0.0175, indicating ß-convergence (Barro and Sala-i-Martin, 1992, Table 1, p. 231). On the basis of the broad cross-country Summers and Heston (1988) data set (1960-85, 98 countries) the authors estimate an unconditional convergence equation which implies a rate of convergence of -0.0037, indicating (unconditional) ß-divergence. Subsequently, the authors estimate a conditional convergence equation, which includes a set of control variables.[179] In this case the rate of convergence turns out to be 0.0184 indicating conditional ß-convergence. Finally, in the case of 20 OECD countries (1960-85) the rate of (conditional) convergence turns out to be 0.0203 (Barro and Sala-i-Martin, 1992, Table 3, p. 242). The authors conclude by noting that the data show conditional ß-convergence at a rate of roughly 2 per cent and that this result is quantitatively consistent with the neoclassical model if the capital share is around 0.8. Economically, this indicates that a broad concept of capital, which includes physical as well as human capital, seems to be appropriate.

Similarly, Mankiw, Romer, and Weil (1992) estimate an unconditional convergence equation using the Summers and Heston (1988) data set for three different samples of countries: 98 non-oil exporting countries, a smaller group of 75 countries (labelled the intermediate sample), and 22 OECD countries (Mankiw, Romer, and Weil, 1992, p. 413). The convergence coefficient is slightly above zero for the non-oil sample and zero for the intermediate sample. However, for the OECD sample the convergence coefficient is significantly negative indicating (conditional) ß-convergence in this case (Mankiw, Romer, and Weil, 1992, Table III, p. 425).[180] Subsequently, the authors estimate a conditional convergence equation where the control vector comprises the investment rate, the population growth rate, and a measure of human capital. The convergence coefficient turns out to be significantly negative for all three samples of countries. The estimates imply a numerical value for the rate of convergence ranging from 0.0137 (non-oil sample) over 0.0182 (intermediate sample) to 0.0203 (OECD sample) (Mankiw, Romer, and Weil, 1992, Table V, p. 426). The authors conclude that (conditional) convergence occurs at approximately the rate

---

[179] These consist in (initial) primary and secondary school enrolment rates, the average ratio of government consumption expenditures to GDP, proxies for political stability, and a measure of market distortions (Barro and Sala-i-Martin, 1992, p. 243).

[180] Mankiw, Romer, and Weil (1992, p. 425) use a specification of the convergence regression which equals $\gamma = x + a\ln[y(0)] + e$. In this case $a < 0$ ($\lambda < 0$) indicates ß-convergence.

predicted by the neoclassical growth model which is explicitly augmented to include human in addition to physical capital.

In summary, a basic finding of the conditional convergence literature is the sharp contrast between the signs of the coefficient on initial per capita income. This result indicates that economies which are positioned further below their balanced-growth path tend to grow faster. In addition, the literature reviewed above claims that the rate of conditional convergence is remarkably stable, at around 2 per cent per year. This result is interpreted as being qualitatively and even quantitatively consistent with the neoclassical theory of growth provided that the capital share is large enough. Therefore, capital is interpreted broadly as including physical as well as human capital, which bears the implication that the returns to this broad concept of capital diminish very slowly (Sala-i-Martin, 1996b, Sections IV/V; Klenow and Rodríguez-Clare, 1997, p. 602; de la Fuente, 1997, pp. 55-58; and Temple, 1999, p. 28).[181]

5.2.3 Some methodological issues

This section discusses some of the methodological issues which arise within the context of cross-sectional conditional convergence analyses. On this occasion three problems will be considered: (i) endogeneity of the control variables; (ii) fixed bias effects due to omitted variables; and (iii) the appropriate calculation of growth rates.[182]

Endogeneity of the control variables

As has been shown in the previous section, the analysis of conditional convergence is crucially based on the approximation of the balanced-growth path. Empirically this is achieved by employing a set of control variables. On account of the definition of the balanced-growth path the control variables are required to be time invariant. However, there are strong theoretical arguments and solid empirical support for the view that at least a subset of the control variables, like the investment rates in physical and human capital as well as the rate of population growth, varies systematically with the level of per capita income (Cohen, 1992, p. 11;

---

[181] The cross-sectional convergence approach has been criticised by several authors; for some of the fundamental criticisms see Quah (1996) and Evans (1997). In addition, it should be noted that several econometric problems like fixed effects, measurement errors, heterogeneity biases, outliers, and endogeneity have been ignored frequently within this literature. Therefore, the results are not entirely reliable as Temple (1999, p. 28) points out. Besides, it should be noted that some recent empirical convergence analyses which use panel data techniques find much higher rates of convergence, i.e. between 6 and 11 per cent (Canova and Marcet, 1995; Islam, 1995; and Caselli, Esquivel, and Lefort, 1996).

[182] Additional econometric problems connected with cross-sectional convergence analyses are discussed more comprehensively in Bohl (1998) and Temple (1999).

Caselli, Esquivel, and Lefort, 1996, p. 367; Cho, 1996, Section 2). The possibility of endogenous control variables causes two distinct problems whereat the first is purely econometric while the second concerns the theoretical interpretation of the conditional convergence results.

The presence of endogeneity means that some of the control variables might be determined simultaneously with the level or the growth rate of per capita income. In this case the control variables are correlated with the error term and the usual ordinary least-squares procedure (OLS) yields biased and inconsistent estimators (Pindyck and Rubinfeld, 1991, pp. 290/291 and Cho, 1996, p. 676). For expositional convenience assume that there is only one control variable and that the 'true' structural convergence model consists of two equations:

$$\gamma_{i,0,t} \equiv [\ln(y_{i,t}) - \ln(y_{i,0})]/t = a_0 - a_1 \ln(y_{i,0}) + a_2 \ln(x_{i,0}) + \varepsilon_{i,0,t} \quad (5.19)$$

$$\ln(x_{i,0}) = b_0 + b_1 \ln(y_{i,0}) + v_{i,0}. \quad (5.20)$$

Now, within the context of empirical convergence analyses, the issue of biased and inconsistent OLS estimators depends heavily on the specification of the control variable (Temple, 1999, p. 22). Mankiw, Romer, and Weil (1992), for example, estimate a convergence regression similar to (5.19) with the control variables specified as averages over the sample period, i.e. $\bar{x}_i = (x_{i,t} + x_{i,0})0.5$. The reason for this procedure is that the control variables are not constant in reality (Mankiw, Romer, and Weil, 1992, pp. 412/413). By substituting $\bar{x}_i$ for $x_{i,0}$ in (5.19), the above equation system becomes simultaneous and the control variable, $\bar{x}_i$, becomes endogenous with respect to the growth rate of per capita income. Consequently, the control variable is correlated with the error term, and OLS estimators are biased and inconsistent.[183] In order to avoid this problem other authors use the initial or lagged values of the control variables as instruments (Barro, 1991, p. 415; Barro and Sala-i-Martin, 1992, p. 243; Barro and Lee, 1994b, pp. 12 and 20/21; Sala-i-Martin, 1996b, p. 1027; additionally Mankiw, 1995, pp. 303/304 and Temple, 1999, pp. 22/23). In this case, the above equation system demonstrates that convergence regressions like (5.19) originate from a recursive system of equations and therefore OLS estimators are unbiased and consistent (Pindyck and Rubinfeld, 1991, p. 298 and de la Fuente, 1997, p. 69). However, it can sensibly be questioned whether the control variables can really be considered as being

---

[183] Mankiw, Romer, and Weil (1992, pp. 411/412) acknowledge that the possible endogeneity of the control variables might cause problems and mention three reasons for the assumption that the saving rate and the rate of population growth are independent from the error term within their specification of convergence regression.

constant along the transition to the balanced-growth equilibrium (Klenow and Rodríguez-Clare, 1997, p. 603). This question can, in principle, be answered on empirical or theoretical grounds. As already mentioned above, empirical evidence clearly suggests that at least the investment rates in physical and human capital and the growth rate of population vary systematically with the level of per capita income (Cohen, 1992, p. 11; Caselli, Esquivel, and Lefort, 1996, p. 367; and Cho, 1996, Section 2). Theoretically, the constancy of the control variables along the transition path seems to represent special cases rather than the rule for the class models with sound microeconomic foundations. For example, the Ramsey-Cass-Koopmans model implies a constant investment rate only if the balanced-growth investment rate equals the intertemporal elasticity of substitution in consumption (e.g. Barro and Sala-i-Martin, 1995, pp. 77-79).[184]

The second point concerns the theoretical interpretation of the conditional convergence results. Similarly to the preceding paragraph, this point is equally rooted in the endogeneity of a subset of the control variables. In this case, the variation of some of the control variables with income contains important information about the transition to the balanced-growth equilibrium rather than about the balanced-growth equilibrium itself. In order to illustrate this point, a general expression for the growth rate of per capita income is considered (Cho, 1996, p. 670):

$$\gamma = G[y, x_1, x_2(y)].$$ (5.21)

The conditional convergence coefficient measures merely the partial correlation between the growth rate of per capita income and the level of per capita income, i.e. $\partial \gamma / \partial y$. However, if some of the control variables vary with per capita income, the total correlation differs from this partial correlation. For the growth rate specification given in (5.21) the total derivative is: $d\gamma / dy = \partial \gamma / \partial y + (\partial \gamma / \partial x_2) \cdot (dx_2 / dy)$. The analysis of (conditional) convergence intends to study comprehensively the transition process to the balanced-growth equilibrium. Consequently, it seems that the convergence question should consider the total correlation including the indirect effects through the endogenous channels of the control variables (Cho, 1996, p. 670 and Klenow and Rodríguez-Clare, 1997,

---

[184] In contrary, there are a lot of theoretical approaches which demonstrate the endogeneity of several typical control variables. For instance, the saving rate can be shown to increase with the level of per capita income in the course of economic development (Chapter 3) and several growth models imply a negative relation between the population growth rate and the level of per capita income (Becker and Barro, 1988 and Becker, Murphy, and Tamura, 1990).

p. 603).[185] In addition, the second component of the total derivative, i.e. $(\partial \gamma / \partial x_2) \cdot (dx_2 / dy)$, contains important information on the transition process and indicates whether growth tends to accelerate or decelerate in the course of economic development. This information can be used to decompose empirically the total correlation between growth and the level of per capita income into mechanisms of (conditional) ß-convergence and ß-divergence (Cho, 1996, pp. 670 and 679).

An omitted variable

Equation (5.14), which shows the time path of the logarithm of per capita income, immediately demonstrates that the initial level of technology, $A(0)$, determines, among other variables, the intercept of the balanced-growth path. Consequently, this variable should, in principle, be included into conditional convergence regressions. However, because this variable cannot be observed directly it is usually omitted.[186] As a result, the parameter estimates are biased provided that the omitted variable is correlated with other right-hand-side variables (Temple, 1998, p. 44). This assumption seems to be highly plausible as Temple (1999, p. 15) points out: "*In practice, countries that are relatively less efficient are also likely to have lower investment rates, and one can easily imagine further correlations with other right-hand-side variables.*"[187] Because international variations in efficiency seem to be most important between different

---

[185] Moreover, Cohen (1992, p. 10) questions whether a balanced-growth path can be identified empirically if the control variables vary in the course of economic development. Therefore, he uses the expression 'pseudo steady state'. Caselli, Esquivel, and Lefort (1996, pp. 367/368) question the concept of exogenous control variables more radically: "*At a more abstract level, we wonder whether the very notion of exogenous variables is at all useful in a growth framework (the only exception is perhaps the morphological structure of a country's geography).*" Barro and Sala-i-Martin (1995, p. 431, fn. 7) acknowledge that the interpretation of the estimated rate of convergence is only correct if "*...the other right hand side variables do not change with per capita income*" and Barro (1997, p. 17, fn. 6) notices that "*[a] full treatment of convergence would also require an analysis of how the various explanatory variables – such as schooling, health, fertility – respond to the development of the economy.*"

[186] Mankiw, Romer, and Weil (1992, p. 424) acknowledge this problem without correcting for it: "*If countries have permanent differences in their production functions - that is, different A(0)'s - then these A(0)'s would enter as part of the error term and would be positively correlated with initial income. Hence, variations in A(0) would bias the coefficient on initial income toward zero.*" In addition, Caselli, Esquivel, and Lefort (1996, p. 364) observe that country-specific effects which represent differences in technology or tastes give rise to omitted variable bias and the usual treatment almost always uses the invalid assumption that such effects are uncorrelated with the other right-hand-side variables.

[187] Islam (1995) and Caselli, Esquivel, and Lefort (1996) present evidence that the initial efficiency is indeed correlated with the regressors.

(sub-)continents, one way to account for this omitted variable problem consists in the use of regional dummy variables. Temple (1998, p. 45) shows that 75 per cent of the variation in initial efficiency are 'explained' by regional dummies.[188]

The calculation of growth rates

The third point concerns the calculation of average growth rates, which are the dependent variable in cross-country growth regressions. The usual method merely uses the figures on initial and final output for each country. However, macroeconomic shocks and business cycle effects are likely to produce deviations from the trend path of output. Therefore, it seems to be preferable to employ the whole time series information contained in the Summers and Heston data set and to estimate a trend path by regressing the whole of the logarithmic per capita income series on a constant and a time trend. On the basis of this fitted trend path in logarithmic per capita income one can easily calculate 'least-square growth rates', which are more robust with respect to short-run instabilities (Temple, 1999, p. 10).

5.3 Cross-sectional convergence analysis

5.3.1 Procedure and data

This section describes the procedure, which will be applied in this section, and the definitions and sources of the data. The procedure is used to identify mechanisms of convergence and divergence and essentially follows a procedure suggested by Cho (1996). The conditional convergence regression which will be estimated is of the following form:[189]

$$\gamma_{i,0,t} = a_0 + a_1 \ln(y_{i,0}) + b_j \ln(\overline{x}_{j,i}) + \varepsilon_{i,0,t}, \tag{5.22}$$

where $\gamma_{i,0,t}$ denotes the average annual growth rate of per capita income for country i over the sample period $[0, t]$, $y_{i,0}$ the initial level of per capita income for country i, $\overline{x}_{j,i}$ the average over the sample period of the j-th control variable for country i, and $\varepsilon_{i,0,t}$ an identically and independ-

---

[188] In addition, Temple (1998, p. 44) stresses that the introduction of regional dummies has the advantage of controlling for variations in technical progress that are not already captured by the control variables.

[189] Cho (1996, p. 671 and fn. 7) uses a non-logarithmic specification for the control variables. However, if the regression equation is considered as resulting from an explicit growth model, all regressors should uniquely have a logarithmic or non-logarithmic specification.

ently distributed error term, respectively. The control variables are considered as being simultaneously determined with the level of per capita income. Consequently, the averages of the control variables over the sample period are specified as being dependent on the average level of per capita income over the sample period:

$$\ln(\overline{x}_{j,i}) = c_0 + c_j \ln(\overline{y}_i) + v_{j,i}.$$ (5.23)

The coefficient c_j gives the elasticity of the average j-th control variable with respect to average per capita income. In order to estimate the conditional convergence regression (5.22) consistently, a two-stage least-square procedure (TSLS) is employed. In addition, the elasticities of the control variables with respect to per capita income are estimated by applying an OLS procedure to the regression equation (5.23).

The underlying data set comprises 120 economies and covers the time period from 1960-85.[190] Following Mankiw, Romer, and Weil (1992) oil-producing countries are excluded from the sample because a large part of recorded GDP for these countries represents the extraction of existing resources and one should not expect standard growth models to account for measured GDP in these countries (Mankiw, Romer, and Weil, 1992, p. 413).[191] The various variables which are utilised within this section are shown in Table 5.1. In addition, this table describes the definitions of variables, their availability, and sources.

As indicated above, the variables are used in logarithmic form.[192] Those variables which can become zero or negative, but smaller than unity in absolute value, are utilised in the form of $\log(1 + \overline{x}_i)$ (e.g. Barro and Lee, 1994b, pp. 16/17 and Barro and Sala-i-Martin, 1995, p. 425). Following Temple (1998) the set of dummy variables consists of regional dummies for sub-Saharan Africa (D1) (Easterly and Levine, 1997, pp. 1242-1245), the group of industrialised countries (D2) (Mankiw, Romer, and Weil, 1992, pp. 434-436), East Asia (D3) (Temple, 1998, p. 62), and Latin America and the Caribbean (D4) (Easterly and Levine, 1997, pp. 1242-

---

[190] More recent data are rarely available for several control variables in the case of DCs. The extension of the sample period would therefore introduce a sample selection bias.

[191] The set of excluded countries comprises Bahrain, Gabon, Iran, Iraq, Kuwait, Oman, Saudi Arabia, and the United Arab Emirates. In addition, Lesotho is excluded because consumption (private and government) far exceeds GDP in every year of the sample, indicating that income from abroad constitutes an extremely large fraction of GDP (Mankiw, Romer, and Weil, 1992, p. 413, fn. 5).

[192] Within the empirical conditional convergence literature some authors use logarithmic variables uniformly (e.g. Mankiw, Romer, and Weil, 1992), while others use non-logarithmic control variables (e.g. Cho, 1996).

Table 5.1. Definitions of variables, availability, and sources

Variable	Definition	Availability (Number of countries)	Source
y	Real GDP per capita	annually (120)	Penn World Tables 5.6[a]
i	Investment share of GDP	annually (119)	Penn World Tables 5.6
n	Population growth rate	annually (117)	Penn World Tables 5.6
h	Educational attainment: average schooling years in total population over age 25	quinquennially (91)	Barro and Lee (1994a)
g	Government share of GDP	annually (120)	Penn World Tables 5.6
p	Measure of political instability consisting of assassinations per million population per year (ass) and the number of revolutions per year (rev): $p = 0.5 \cdot ass + 0.5 \cdot rev$	annually (83)	Banks (1997)
b	Black-market premium	averages over five year sub-periods (96)	Barro and Lee (1994a)
f	Financial development measured as domestic credit provided by banking sector as share of GDP	annually (63)	World Bank (1998)

[a] This data set is referred as Summers and Heston (1999), which is basically described and discussed in Summers and Heston (1988, 1991).

1245). Finally, the dependent variables of the conditional convergence regression are least-square growth rates as explained in Section 5.2.3. Fig. 5.3 (a) shows the histogram for the actual growth rates of per capita income and Fig. 5.3 (b) shows the histogram for the least-square growth rates. The vertical axes show the number of countries (no.), while the horizontal axes show the annual average growth rates over the sample period 1960-85 (gry).

This section extends Cho's (1996) paper in three directions: (i) The set of control variables is enlarged. In addition to the investment rate and the rate of population growth, the government share of GDP, the black-market premium on foreign exchange, a proxy for human capital, a measure of political instability, and a measure of financial development are considered. (ii) The possibility of international differences in the initial level of efficiency is taken into consideration by the use of regional dummy variables. (iii) The dependent variable are least-square growth rates instead of actual growth rates.

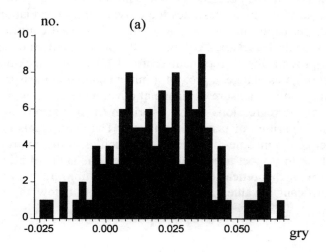

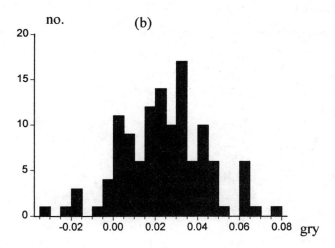

Fig. 5.3. Histograms for actual and least-square growth rates, 1960-85

5.3.2 Endogeneity of control variables

It has been argued in Section 5.2.3 that the control variables are likely to depend systematically on the level of per capita income. In this case those variables which are expected to proxy the balanced-growth path vary during the transition to the balanced-growth equilibrium. This section presents empirical evidence which illustrates the cross-country correlation between the level of per capita income and a set of widely used control variables. This set of control variables comprises the investment rate, the rate of population growth, the government share of GDP, the black-market premium on foreign exchange, a proxy for human capital, a measure of political instability, and a measure of financial development. Table 5.2 presents the results of the regressions of the logarithm of the various control variables on the logarithm of per capita income. The coefficients of the logarithm of per capita income represent the elasticities of the control variables under study with respect to per capita income. The signs of all elasticities are in line with theoretical expectations. In addition, all coefficients are highly significant (t-values are shown in brackets below the coefficient estimates).

Table 5.2. Endogenous control variables

Dependent variable	Constant[*]	$\ln(\bar{y})$ [*]	R^2	Sample size
$\ln(\bar{i})$	-5.62 (-14.84)	0.478 (9.76)	0.45	119
$\ln(\bar{n})$	-0.66 (-1.70)	-0.442 (-8.80)	0.40	117
$\ln(\bar{g})$	-0.43 (-1.60)	-0.175 (-5.01)	0.17	120
$\ln(1+\bar{b})$	1.32 (5.98)	-0.143 (-5.04)	0.22	93
$\ln(\bar{h})$	-3.94 (-10.36)	0.655 (13.70)	0.69	87
$\ln(1+\bar{p})$	0.39 (5.17)	-0.040 (-4.18)	0.18	83
$\ln(1+\bar{f})$	-0.56 (-3.53)	0.114 (5.77)	0.35	63

[*]t-values are shown in brackets below the coefficient estimates.

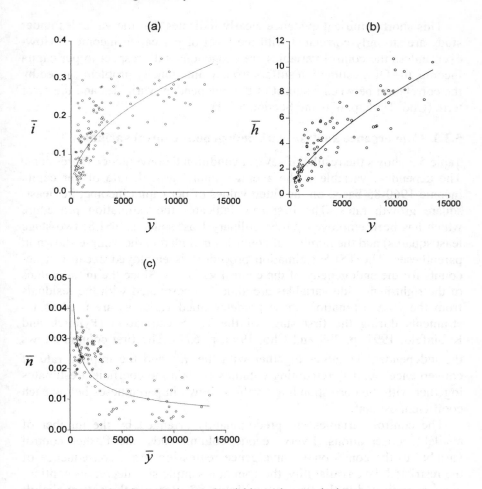

Fig. 5.4. Scatter plots for several control variables and per capita income

The correlation between some of the control variables and the level of per capita income is illustrated graphically. Fig. 5.4 shows scatter plots for the averages of three control variables and the average of per capita income over the sample period 1960-85. In addition, each diagram contains a log-linear regression line. The investment rate and the proxy for human capital appear to vary positively with the level of per capita income [Fig. 5.4 (a) and (b)], while the population growth rate appears to vary negatively with the level of per capita income [Fig. 5.4 (c)].

This short empirical evidence clearly indicates that the variables under study are strongly correlated with the level of per capita income.[193] However, unless the control variables are exogenous with respect to per capita income, the OLS estimation suffers from a simultaneity problem caused by the correlation between a subset of the independent variables and the error term (Cho, 1996, p. 676 and Section 5.2.3).

5.3.3 Convergence analysis with endogenous control variables

Table 5.3 shows the results of several conditional convergence regressions. The dependent variable is the average annual growth rate of per capita income 1960-85 based on the fitted values of per capita income, i.e. least-square growth rates. The first row indicates the estimation procedure which has been employed (OLS: ordinary least squares, TSLS: two-stage least squares) and the number of countries included in the sample shown in parentheses. The TSLS estimation procedure is employed because it accounts for the endogeneity of the control variables. Since the initial values of the right-hand-side variables are almost uncorrelated with the residuals from the OLS estimation, these predetermined variables are used as instruments during the first stage of the TSLS estimation (Pyndick and Rubinfeld, 1991, p. 299 and Cho, 1996, p. 677). The first column shows the independent variables together with the R^2 and the implied rate of convergence, λ. The remaining columns contain the coefficient estimates together with the corresponding t-values shown in parentheses below each coefficient estimate.

The control variables are predominantly arranged by the number of available observations. Every second column adds one further control variable to the conditional convergence regression. As a consequence of the restricted data availability, the common sample size decreases continuously as indicated in the first row of Table 5.3. Because the data availability is higher for 'rich' countries compared to 'poor' countries, the diminishing sample size inevitably introduces a sample selection bias. Therefore, the interpretations of the next section are based on the coefficient estimates which stem from the regression with the tallest sample size. Because some

---

[193] This correlation suggests that the control variables, $\bar{x}_j$, are equally correlated with the initial level of per capita income, $y_{i,0}$ (Cho, 1996, Section 2). The fact that some of the right-hand-side variables are highly correlated with each other means that the issue of multicollinearity arises. Under standard econometric assumptions the OLS coefficient estimates are nonetheless unbiased. However, the standard errors of the coefficient estimates are biased upward (Pindyck and Rubinfeld, 1991, p. 84 and Mankiw, 1995, pp. 304-306).

Table 5.3. Convergence regression results
Dependent variable: average annual least-square growth rate of per capita income 1960-85.

	OLS (116)	OLS (116)	TSLS (112)	TSLS (112)	TSLS (90)	TSLS (90)	TSLS (75)	TSLS (75)	TSLS (61)	TSLS (61)	TSLS (45)	TSLS (45)
Constant	0.09723 (4.77)	0.09795 (5.29)	0.08299 (3.68)	0.06816 (3.17)	0.11910 (4.29)	0.07449 (2.60)	0.10887 (4.23)	0.08358 (3.01)	0.12269 (4.97)	0.11861 (4.25)	0.13434 (3.84)	0.14234 (4.15)
$\ln[y(60)]$	-0.00927 (-3.60)	-0.01025 (-4.21)	-0.00646 (-2.25)	-0.00472 (-1.59)	-0.00923 (-2.72)	-0.00595 (-1.55)	-0.01122 (-3.03)	-0.01145 (-2.72)	-0.01100 (-3.06)	-0.01492 (-4.08)	-0.01405 (-3.45)	-0.01511 (-4.58)
$\ln(\bar{i})$	0.01561 (6.42)	0.01973 (7.68)	0.00987 (3.29)	0.01306 (4.12)	0.00819 (2.24)	0.01245 (3.02)	0.00450 (0.91)	0.00791 (1.34)	0.01653 (3.42)	0.01571 (2.61)	0.01282 (1.65)	0.01552 (1.77)
$\ln(\bar{n})$	-0.00377 (-1.42)	-0.00464 (-1.70)	-0.00063 (-0.17)	-0.00057 (-0.16)	0.00349 (0.84)	0.00056 (0.14)	0.00057 (0.16)	-0.00217 (-0.57)	-0.00217 (-0.78)	-0.00429 (-1.39)	-0.00030 (-0.08)	-0.00463 (-1.58)
$\ln(\bar{g})$	-0.00954 (-2.44)	-0.01184 (-2.87)	-0.00624 (-1.25)	-0.00749 (-1.43)	-0.00758 (-1.16)	-0.01144 (-1.67)	-0.00904 (-1.38)	-0.01418 (-2.09)	-0.00685 (-1.28)	-0.01374 (-2.44)	-0.00231 (-0.39)	-0.00306 (-0.55)
$\ln(1+\bar{b})$					-0.01705 (-1.56)	-0.00002 (-0.00)	-0.02144 (-1.89)	-0.00682 (-0.49)	-0.00769 (-0.89)	-0.00343 (-0.33)	0.00483 (0.31)	-0.01564 (-1.71)
$\ln(\bar{h})$							0.00566 (1.29)	0.00736 (1.42)	0.00091 (0.24)	0.00566 (1.22)	0.00011 (0.02)	0.00416 (0.76)
$\ln(1+\bar{p})$									-0.00114 (-0.05)	-0.02357 (-0.94)	0.01028 (0.33)	-0.01747 (-0.57)
$\ln(1+\bar{f})$											0.00553 (0.33)	-0.00049 (-0.02)
D1	-0.01340 (-3.37)		-0.01501 (-3.58)		-0.01787 (-3.74)		-0.01788 (-3.82)		-0.01927 (-4.08)		-0.02262 (-0.99)	
D2	-0.00474 (-0.89)		-0.00080 (-0.13)		0.00253 (0.37)		-0.00335 (-0.49)		-0.00301 (-0.53)		0.02353 (1.85)	
D3	0.01874 (2.80)		0.02288 (3.19)		0.01759 (2.18)		0.01406 (1.76)		0.01373 (1.96)		0.02815 (2.84)	
D4	-0.01168 (-2.72)		-0.01090 (-2.40)		-0.01423 (-2.71)		-0.01586 (-3.02)		-0.01059 (-2.48)		0.00458 (0.73)	
R^2	0.56	0.42	0.53	0.37	0.58	0.37	0.67	0.45	0.75	0.59	0.68	0.66
implied λ	0.01054	0.01184	0.00704	0.00502								

of the control variables are correlated with the dummy variables, each regression is reestimated by excluding the dummy variables.[194]

5.3.4 Interpretation of main findings

First of all, most of the regressions show a comparably high R^2, i.e. the
goodness of fit is remarkable (Table 5.3, last row but one). The second and
the fourth column of Table 5.3 show that the dummy variable for sub-
Saharan Africa, D1, as well as the dummy variable for Latin America and
the Caribbean, D4, are significantly negative and that the dummy variable
for East Asia, D3, is significantly positive.[195] For six of the eight right-
hand-side variables, excluding the constant and the dummy variables, the
signs are in line with the theoretical expectations. The coefficient of the
political-instability variable, p, shows the 'wrong' sign and is insignificant. The coefficient of the financial-development variable, f, also appears with the 'wrong' sign and is insignificant when the regional dummies are excluded. Therefore, these variables are excluded from the following interpretation.

The second column of Table 5.3 reproduces an important result of the
empirical convergence literature. The convergence coefficient which results from a conditional convergence estimation is significantly negative,
the numerical value amounts to -0.00927 and the corresponding t-value is -
3.60 (Table 5.3, second column). Therefore, the conditional convergence
hypothesis of the neoclassical growth model is supported. The implied rate
of convergence amounts to 1 per cent (Table 5.3, last row) and is roughly
consistent with the usual results of the cross-sectional convergence literature (see Section 5.2.2). The fourth column reports the estimation results
using a TSLS procedure. In this case, the estimated convergence coefficient is higher, i.e. smaller in absolute value, and amounts to -0.00646
(Table 5.3, fourth column).[196] Accordingly, an increase in the initial level of
per capita income by 1 per cent is estimated to reduce the average annual
growth rate of per capita income by approximately 0.6 percentage points

[194] The correlation between some of the control variables and the regional dummies, i.e.
multicollinearity, causes a problem for the interpretation of the regression coefficients. One
possibility to handle this problem is the elimination of regressors (Rinne, 1976, p. 103 and
Pindyck and Rubinfeld, 1991, p. 84).
[195] This indicates that some determinants which are relevant to growth for these groups of
countries are not captured adequately by the list of right-hand-side variables (Barro and
Sala-i-Martin, 1995, pp. 443/444 and Levine and Renelt, 1992, p. 949). Easterly and Levine
(1997), for example, analyse the meaning of ethnic diversity in sub-Saharan Africa for the
process of growth.
[196] The comparison of the convergence coefficients from column two and column four
illustrates the downward estimation bias which is caused by the endogeneity of the control
variables (Cho, 1996, p. 676).

on average. The implied speed of convergence is 0.7 per cent. However, this interpretation crucially relies on the assumption that the other explanatory variables are held constant (Barro and Sala-i-Martin, 1995, p. 431). In addition, this convergence effect should be interpreted carefully as representing the net effect of all unidentified convergence mechanisms, including the neoclassical convergence mechanism as well as the technological catch-up mechanism, and divergence mechanisms (de la Fuente, 1997, pp. 62/63).

In what follows the estimation results from Table 5.2 are combined with the estimation results from Table 5.3 in order to determine numerically several mechanisms of convergence or divergence. Formally, various coefficients of the control variables from the conditional convergence regression, $\partial \gamma / \partial \ln(\bar{x}_i)$, are combined with the corresponding elasticities of the control variables with respect to per capita income, $d\ln(\bar{x}_i)/d\ln(\bar{y})$.

The resulting coefficient, $CM_j \equiv \dfrac{\partial \gamma}{\partial \ln(\bar{x}_j)} \cdot \dfrac{d\ln(\bar{x}_j)}{d\ln(\bar{y})}$, describes the change in the growth rate of per capita income caused by an increase in the level of per capita income by accounting for the endogenous variation of the control variables. This coefficient describes a *mechanism of conditional β-convergence* if $CM_j < 0$ and a *mechanism of conditional β-divergence* if $CM_j > 0$.

The fourth column in Table 5.3 shows that the partial correlation between the growth rate of per capita income and the investment rate amounts to 0.00987. An increase in the investment rate by 1 per cent is estimated to increase the growth rate of per capita income by approximately 1 percentage point on average.[197] Table 5.2 shows that the elasticity of the investment rate with respect to per capita income equals 0.478 and,

consequently, $CM_{\bar{i}} \equiv \dfrac{\partial \gamma}{\partial \ln(\bar{i})} \cdot \dfrac{d\ln(\bar{i})}{d\ln(\bar{y})} \cong 0.00987 \cdot 0.478 \cong 0.005$.   This

positive value indicates an important divergence mechanism, which can economically be interpreted in the sense of the subsistence-divergence mechanism analysed in Chapter 3. In the course of economic development, the level of per capita income and the ability to save increase. As a consequence, the saving and investment rate rise as well, which causes the growth rate of per capita income to increase. This mechanism is statisti-

---

[197] It should be noted that other studies find even higher values for this coefficient (e.g. Barro and Sala-i-Martin, 1995, p. 425 and Cho, 1996, p. 679). Table 5.3 (fifth column) shows that this coefficient increases substantially if the regional dummies are omitted.

cally significant since both components of $CM_{\bar{i}}$ are highly significant.[198] Furthermore, the magnitude of this subsistence-divergence mechanism is quantitatively comparable to the conditional convergence mechanism described above.

According to Table 5.3 (fourth column) and Table 5.2 (third row), the 'convergence mechanism' associated with the endogenous variation of the population growth rate is $CM_{\bar{n}} \cong -0.00063 \cdot -0.442 \cong 0.0002$. Because $CM_{\bar{n}} > 0$, the variation in the population growth rate represents a further divergence mechanism. However, the quantitative meaning appears to be small and the statistical significance is extremely fragile.[199]

The partial correlation between the growth rate of per capita income and the government share of GDP (Table 5.3, fourth column) together with the elasticity of the government share of GDP with respect to per capita income (Table 5.2, fourth row) yield the 'convergence mechanism' associated with the government share of GDP: $CM_{\bar{g}} \cong -0.00624 \cdot -0.175 \cong 0.001$. The negative effect of the government share of GDP on growth can be interpreted as the adverse impact of non-productive government expenditures, including military expenditures, as well as the adverse impact of taxation (Levine and Renelt, 1992, pp. 949-953 and Barro and Lee, 1994b, p. 19). Again, the endogenous variation of the government share of GDP establishes a further divergence mechanism.[200]

According to Table 5.3 (sixth column) a decreasing black-market premium is estimated to increase the growth rate of per capita income and according to Table 5.2 (fifth row), the black-market premium falls with the level of per capita income. The corresponding 'convergence mechanism' reads $CM_{\bar{b}} \cong -0.01705 \cdot -0.143 \cong 0.0024$.[201] The black-market premium

---

[198] The t-value of the elasticity of $\bar{i}$ with respect to $\bar{y}$ is 9.76 (Table 5.2, second row) and the t-value of the partial correlation between the growth rate of per capita income and $\ln(\bar{i})$ is 3.29 (Table 5.3, fourth column).

[199] The elasticity of $\bar{n}$ with respect to $\bar{y}$ is significantly negative, the corresponding t-value is -8.80 (Table 5.2, third row). However, the t-value of the coefficient of the population growth rate in the convergence regression merely amounts to -0.17 (Table 5.3, fourth column).

[200] The elasticity of $\bar{g}$ with respect to $\bar{y}$ is significant, the corresponding t-value is -5.01 (Table 5.2, fourth row). However, the coefficient of $\ln(\bar{g})$ in the convergence regression is not significant, the corresponding t-value is -1.25 (Table 5.3, fourth column).

[201] The elasticity of $1+\bar{b}$ with respect to $\bar{y}$ is highly significant, the corresponding t-value is -5.04 (Table 5.2, fifth row). However, the coefficient of $1+\bar{b}$ in the convergence regression is not significant, the corresponding t-value is -1.56 (Table 5.3, sixth column).

can be considered to proxy for government distortions of markets which influence the process of growth adversely (Barro and Sala-i-Martin, 1995, p. 435).

With respect to the human-capital variable, the 'convergence mechanism' reads as follows: $CM_{\bar{h}} \cong 0.00566 \cdot 0.655 \cong 0.004$. This divergence mechanism can be considered as representing a complement to the subsistence-divergence mechanism described above. A rise in the level of per capita income increases the ability to save and hence investment in both physical as well as human capital.[202] The magnitude of this divergence effect is considerable. It is as large as the divergence mechanism resulting from an increase in the investment rate and nearly as large as the conditional convergence mechanism described above.[203]

In summary, a 1 per cent increase in the average level of per capita income over the sample period is estimated to increase the average annual growth rate of per capita income by 1.1 percentage points on average; the extremely fragile divergence mechanism due to $\bar{n}$ has been excluded. This overall divergence effect is quantitatively more important than the convergence effect which results from a rise in the initial level of per capita income. As a consequence, the consideration of the endogenous variation of the control variables implies that the data support conditional ß-divergence instead of conditional ß-convergence, i.e. the growth dynamics seem to be characterised by *unconditional as well as conditional β-divergence*. This interpretation sharply contrasts with the conditional convergence results which state that the growth rate of per capita income falls along the transition path to the balanced-growth equilibrium (Cho, 1996, p. 679). However, this finding has to be interpreted carefully because of the following reasons: (i) The convergence regression only includes a restricted number of control variables. Levine and Renelt (1992) analyse the robustness of the partial correlations within the cross-sectional convergence regression framework and find that most control variables are not robust to changes in the set of control variables. (ii) The only 'convergence mechanism' which appears to be statistically significant in the sense that both components are highly significant is $CM_{\bar{i}}$. With respect to $\bar{g}$, $\bar{b}$, and $\bar{h}$ the mechanisms appear statistically fragile because the partial correlations with the growth rate are not significant at usual significance levels. However, because mul-

---

[202] It should be noted that the human-capital proxy used here is a measure for the stock of human capital rather than a measure for the investment in human capital (Barro and Lee, 1993, Section 3).

[203] The elasticity of $\bar{h}$ with respect to $\bar{y}$ is highly significant, the corresponding t-value is 13.70 (Table 5.2, sixth row). However, the t-value of the coefficient of the human-capital variable in the convergence regression is merely 1.29 (Table 5.3, eighth column). This coefficient increases if the regional dummies are omitted.

ticollinearity is likely to be present within cross-country growth regressions the standard deviations appear to be biased upwards. As a result, the coefficients could be judged as being insignificant although they might be significant (Pyndick and Rubinfeld, 1991, p. 84 and Mankiw, 1995, pp. 304-306).[204] (iii) The restricted data availability inevitably introduces a sample-selection bias because the availability of data is typically correlated with the level of economic development.

5.4 Summary and conclusion

Several influential development and growth theories stressed the notion that, from a theoretical point of view, 'poor' countries are expected to catch up with 'rich' countries. At least two basic economic mechanisms have been discussed in support of this view: (i) Diminishing returns to the factors that can be accumulated cause the growth rate of per capita income to fall in the course of economic development; the neoclassical convergence mechanism. (ii) According to the advantages-of-backwardness hypothesis (Gerschenkron, 1952), 'poor' countries should be able to exploit the opportunity to imitate technologies which have been developed elsewhere. Consequently, 'poor' countries are expected to catch up with 'rich' countries; the technological catching-up mechanism (Abramovitz, 1986). However, advocates of the endogenous growth theory argued convincingly that the convergence hypothesis has to be rejected on empirical grounds (Romer, 1986, Section III). The advocates of the neoclassical growth theory forcefully argued in response that the neoclassical model does imply conditional convergence instead of unconditional convergence (Barro, 1991 and Mankiw, Romer, and Weil, 1992). According to this view, the balanced-growth equilibrium of each country is determined by a set of country-specific variables, the control variables, and the growth rate of per capita income is inversely related to the distance between an economy's current position and its balanced-growth equilibrium. Provided that the balanced-growth path is reached from below, the growth rate should fall during the transition process. However, this interpretation is crucially based on the assumption that control variables are exogenous with respect to the process of economic development. If, on the other hand, the control

---

[204] Multicollinearity is probably present because of two reasons: (i) the endogenous variation of the control variables with per capita income probably shows up as a correlation between the averages of the control variables with the initial level of per capita income for a cross-section of countries (Cho, 1996, pp. 672/673). (ii) The second reason for multicollinearity among a subset of the control variables simply is that "*As a rough approximation, those countries that do things right do most things right, and those countries that do things wrong do most things wrong.*" Mankiw (1995, p. 304).

variables are considered as being endogenous and consequently vary in the course of economic development, then several distinct mechanisms of conditional convergence and divergence are possible. Theoretically, it is unclear *a priori* whether the net 'convergence mechanism' leads to conditional ß-convergence or conditional ß-divergence. The empirical results presented in the preceding section indicate that the growth dynamics of the real world are characterised by unconditional as well as conditional ß-divergence.

6 Summary and conclusion

Four stylised facts of aggregate economic growth, which are primarily relevant to DCs, are set up initially in Chapter 2. This list of stylised facts comprises: (i) a considerable diversity in growth rates of per capita income; (ii) a positive correlation between the saving rate and per capita income; (iii) ß-divergence; and (iv) a hump-shaped growth pattern. The process of growth is moreover interpreted to represent a transition process to a balanced-growth equilibrium, which might take a long period of time. Against this background the process of economic growth is analysed theoretically and empirically within the main chapters.

The fundamental importance of subsistence consumption for the process of growth is investigated in Chapter 3. The linear growth model with Stone-Geary preferences implies an increasing ability to save. As a result, the saving rate rises in the course of economic development. This simple model demonstrates an important mechanism of (conditional) ß-divergence, which has been labelled the subsistence-divergence mechanism. The rate of convergence is extraordinarily low at early stages of economic development and the time span required for the transition towards the asymptotic balanced-growth equilibrium is therefore correspondingly long. The diversity in growth rates can hence be interpreted as representing a transition phenomenon. An extension of this model by diminishing marginal returns to the factors that can be accumulated enables a potential explanation of the hump-shaped growth pattern. The interaction between the subsistence-divergence mechanism and the neoclassical convergence mechanism produces an acceleration of growth subsequently followed by a deceleration.

Chapter 4 deals with the meaning of the productive-consumption hypothesis for the intertemporal consumption trade-off and the process of growth. This hypothesis states that consumption satisfies current needs and simultaneously increases the productive potential of labour. Two basic models with productive consumption are distinguished: Within the human-capital model productive consumption is interpreted as enhancing the stock of human capital, whereas within the labour-efficiency model productive consumption is considered as increasing the efficiency of labour. Both models imply a bias against saving which is especially marked for low levels of per capita income and vanishes as per capita income grows without bound. As a result, the effective intertemporal elasticity of substitution as well as the saving rate increase monotonically in the course of economic development. This implication represents a general result since it does not depend on specific functions or specific sets of parameters. In addition, the simulation shows that the labour-efficiency model can potentially explain the non-monotonic dynamics of the growth rate of per capita income. A hump-shaped pattern of growth specifically occurs, which implies (conditional) ß-divergence for the lower range of per capita income and (conditional) ß-convergence for the higher range of per capita income. One further implication is worth noting at this point: The labour-efficiency model implies that the marginal product of capital is comparatively low at early stages of economic development. The economic reason is simply that capital is combined with a comparatively small amount of labour in units of efficiency because the efficiency of labour is determined endogenously by consumption. This implication is in line with the empirical observation of comparably small differences in the rate of return between 'poor' and 'rich' countries.

In Chapter 5 the process of growth, interpreted as representing mainly transitional dynamics, is empirically analysed by means of cross-sectional conditional convergence regressions. This method is crucially based on the concept of exogenous control variables. However, there are strong theoretical arguments and solid empirical support for the view that at least a subset of the control variables systematically varies in the course of economic development. In addition to econometric issues, the explicit consideration of endogenous control variables affects the theoretical interpretation of the conditional convergence results. Accordingly, the variation of some of the control variables with the level and growth rate of per capita income contains important information about the transition to the balanced-growth equilibrium rather than information about the balanced-growth equilibrium itself. The results indicate that empirical growth processes are just as well characterised by unconditional as by conditional ß-divergence. An important mechanism of conditional ß-divergence is furthermore revealed in addition to the empirically well known neoclassical mechanism of conditional ß-convergence. Specifically, investment in physical and human capital is estimated to increase with per capita income, which in turn leads to a rising growth rate. This result is consistent with the subsistence-divergence mechanism described in Chapter 3 and the divergence mechanism caused by a rise in the saving rate as a result of productive consumption as analysed in Chapter 4.

The study in hand suggests at least two directions for future research. First, the notion of productive consumption can be applied to the consumption of time and can be incorporated into the analysis of time-allocation decisions. This way of reasoning suggests that productive consumption might also be important for developed economies. Second, the growth dynamics of the real world can be considered to be simultaneously affected by distinct mechanisms of (conditional) ß-convergence and ß-divergence. It is of major importance to understand the forces that induce a rise or fall in the growth rate of per capita income along the transition to the balanced-growth equilibrium. The theoretical identification of these mechanisms as implied by the main models of growth would undoubtedly enhance our understanding of the growth process. Moreover, the empirical identification of the mechanisms of ß-convergence and ß-divergence is still in its infancy. In order to exploit the information contained in the data more efficiently, panel data techniques as well as time series techniques can be used for this task.

7 References

Abramovitz, Moses (1986), Catching Up, Forging Ahead, and Falling Behind, *Journal of Economic History*, Vol. XLVI, 385-406.

Aghevli, Bijan B., James M. *Boughton*, Peter J. *Montiel*, Delano *Villanueva*, and George *Woglom* (1990), The Role of National Saving in the World Economy – Recent Trends and Prospects, *IMF Occasional Paper*, No. 67, Washington DC.

Arthur, Brian W., Yu M. *Ermoliev*, and Yu M. *Kaniovski* (1987), Path-Dependent Processes and the Emergence of Macro Structure, *European Journal of Operational Research*, Vol. 30, 294-303.

Atkeson, Andrew and Masao *Ogaki* (1996), Wealth-Varying Intertemporal Elasticities of Substitution: Evidence from Panel and Aggregate Data, *Journal of Monetary Economics*, Vol. 38, 507-534.

Atkinson, Anthony B. (1987), Poverty, The New Palgrave Economic Dictionary, No. 3, London-Basingstoke, 928-933.

Azariadis, Costas (1996), The Economics of Poverty Traps, Part One: Complete Markets, *Journal of Economic Growth*, Vol. 1, 449-486.

Azariadis, Costas and Allan *Drazen* (1990), Threshold Externailities in Economic Development, *Quarterly Journal of Economics*, Vol. 105, 501-526.

Balke, Nathan S. and Thomas B. *Fomby* (1991), Shifting Trends, Segmented Trends, and Infrequent Permanent Shocks, *Journal of Monetary Economics*, Vol. 28, 61-85.

Banks, Arthur S. (1997), Cross-National Time-Series Data Archive, Center for Social Analysis, State University of New York at Binghamton, Binghamton, New York.

Barro, Robert J. (1990), Government Spending in a Simple Model of Endogenous Growth, *Journal of Political Economy*, Vol. 98, S103-S125.

Barro, Robert J. (1991), Economic Growth in a Cross Section of Countries, *Quarterly Journal of Economics*, Vol. 106, 407-443.

Barro, Robert J. (1997), Determinants of Economic Growth: A Cross-Country Empirical Study, MIT Press, Cambridge MA.

Barro, Robert J. and Jong-Wha *Lee* (1993), International Comparisons of Educational Attainment, *Journal of Monetary Economics*, Vol. 32, 363-394.

Barro, Robert J. and Jong-Wha *Lee* (1994a), Data Set for a Panel of 138 Countries, Manuscript, Harvard University.

Barro, Robert J. and Jong-Wha *Lee* (1994b), Sources of Economic Growth, *Carnegie-Rochester Conference Series on Public Policy*, Vol. 40, 1-46.

Barro, Robert J. and Xavier *Sala-i-Martin* (1992), Convergence, *Journal of Political Economy*, Vol. 100, 223-251.

Barro, Robert J. and Xavier X. *Sala-i-Martin* (1995), Economic Growth, McGraw Hill, New York.

Baumol, William J. (1986), Productivity Growth, Convergence, and Welfare: What the Long-Run Data Show, *American Economic Review*, Vol. 76, 1072-1085.

Baumol, William, Sue A. B. **Blackman**, and Edward N. **Wolff** (1989), Productivity and American Leadership: The Long View, MIT Press, Cambridge MA.

Becker, Gary S. (1965), A Theory of Allocation of Time, *Economic Journal*, Vol. 75, 493-517.

Becker, Gary S. (1971), The Economic Approach to Human Behaviour, Part 1: The Economic Approach to Human Behaviour, The University of Chicago Press, Chicago.

Becker, Gary S. and Robert J. **Barro** (1988), A Reformulation of the Economic Theory of Fertility, *Quarterly Journal of Economics*, Vol. 103, 1-25.

Becker, Gary S. and Kevin M. **Murphy** (1988), A Theory of Rational Addiction, *Journal of Political Economy*, Vol. 96, 675-700.

Becker, Gary S., Kevin M. **Murphy**, and Robert **Tamura** (1990), Human Capital, Fertility, and Economic Growth, *Journal of Political Economy*, Vol. 98, S12-S37.

Behrman Jere R. and Anil B. **Deolalikar** (1988), Health and Nutrition, Handbook of Development Economics, Volume II, H. Chenery and T. N. Srinivasan (eds.), Elsevier Science Publishers, Amsterdam, 631-711.

Ben-David, Dan (1994), Convergence Clubs and Diverging Economies, *CEPR Discussion Papers*, No. 922.

Benhabib, Jess and Jordi **Gali** (1995), On Growth and Indeterminacy: Some Theory and Evidence, *Carnegie-Rochester Conference Series on Public Policy*, Vol. 43, 163-211.

Blanchard, Oliver J. and Stanley **Fischer** (1989), Lectures on Macroeconomics, MIT Press, Cambridge MA.

Blaug, Mark (1987), Productive and Unproductive Consumption, The New Palgrave: A Dictionary of Economics, J. Eatwell, M. Milgate, P. Newman (eds.), The Macmillan Press, New York, 1007-1008.

Blaug, Mark (1992), The Methodology of Economics, Or How Economists Explain, Cambridge University Press, Cambridge MA.

Bliss, Christopher and Nicholas **Stern** (1978), Productivity, Wages and Nutrition, Part I: The Theory, *Journal of Development Economics*, Vol. 5, 331-362.

Bohl, Martin T. (1998), Konvergenz westdeutscher Regionen? Neue empirische Ergebnisse auf der Basis von Panel-Einheitswurzeltests, *Konjunkturpolitik*, Vol. 44, 82-99.

Canova, Fabio and Albert **Marcet** (1995), The Poor stay Poor: Non-Convergence across Countries and Regions, *CEPR Discussion Paper*, No. 1265.

Caselli, Francesco, Gerardo **Esquivel**, and Fernando **Lefort** (1996), Reopening the Convergence Debate: A New Look at Cross-Country Growth Empirics, *Journal of Economic Growth*, Vol. 1, 363-389.

Cass, David (1965), Optimum Growth in an Aggregative Model of Capital Accumulation, *Review of Economic Studies*, Vol. 32, 233-240.

Chiang, Alpha C. (1984), Fundamental Methods of Mathematical Economics, McGraw Hill, New York.

Cho, Dongchul (1994), Industrialization, Convergence, and Patterns of Growth, *Southern Economic Journal*, Vol. 61, 398-414.

Cho, Dongchul (1996), An Alternative Interpretation of the Conditional Convergence Results, *Journal of Money, Credit and Banking*, Vol. 28, 669-681.

Christiano, Lawrence (1989), Understanding Japan's Saving Rate: The Reconstruction Hypothesis, *Federal Reserve of Minneapolis Quarterly Review*, Spring, 10-15.

Chung, Jae Wan (1994), Utility and Production Functions: Theory and Applications, Blackwell Publishers, Cambridge MA.

Cohen, Daniel (1992), Tests of the 'Convergence Hypothesis': A Critical Note, *CEPR Discussion Paper*, No. 691.

de la Fuente, Angel (1997), The Empirics of Growth and Convergence: A Selective Review, *Journal of Economic Dynamics and Control*, Vol. 21, 23-73.

De Long, Bradford J. (1988), Productivity Growth, Convergence, and Welfare: Comment, *American Economic Review*, Vol. 78, 1138-1154.

Deolalikar, Anil B. (1988), Nutrition and Labor Productivity in Agriculture: Estimates for Rural South India, *The Review of Economics & Statistics*, Vol. 60, 406-413.

Dollar, David (1992), Exploiting the Advantages of Backwardness: The Importance of Education and Outward Orientation, World Bank, Washington DC.

Dorfman, Robert (1969), An Economic Interpretation of Optimal Control Theory, *American Economic Review*, Vol. 59, 817-831.

Durlauf, Steven N. and Danny T. *Quah* (1998), The New Empirics of Economic Growth, *Centre for Economic Performance Discussion Paper*, No. 384.

Easterly, William (1994), Economic Stagnation, Fixed Factors, and Policy Thresholds, *Journal of Monetary Economics*, Vol. 33, 525-557.

Easterly, William and Ross *Levine* (1997), Africa's Growth Tragedy: Policies and Ethnic Divisions, *Quarterly Journal of Economics*, Vol. CXII, 1203-1250.

Easterly, William, Robert *King*, Ross *Levine*, and Sergio *Rebelo* (1992), How Do National Policies Affect Long-Run Growth?, *World Bank Discussion Papers* No. 164, World Bank, Washington DC.

Evans, Paul (1997), How Fast Do Economies Converge?, *Review of Economics and Statistics*, Vol. 79, 219-225.

Feichtinger, Gustav and Richard F. *Hartl* (1986), Optimale Kontrolle ökonomischer Prozesse: Anwendung des Maximumprinzips in den Wirtschaftswissenschaften, de Gruyter, Berlin.

Fisher, Franklin M. (1987), Aggregation Problem, The New Palgrave: A Dictionary of Economics, J. Eatwell, M. Milgate, P. Newman (eds.), The Macmillan Press, New York, 53-55.

Fisher, Irving (1907), The Rate of Interest, Macmillan, New York.

Fogel, Robert W. (1994), Economic Growth, Population Theory, and Physiology: The Bearing of Long-Term Processes on the Making of Economic Policy, *American Economic Review*, Vol. 84, 369-395.

Friedman, Milton (1953), The Methodology of Positive Economics, in Essays in Positive Economics, University of Chicago Press, Chicago.

Gandolfo, Giancarlo (1996), Economic Dynamics, Springer-Verlag, Berlin.

Geary, Robert C. (1950), A Note on 'A Constant Utility Index of the Cost of Living', *Review of Economic Studies*, Vol. 18, 65-66.

Gerschenkron, Alexander (1952), Economic Backwardness in Historical Perspective, Bert F. Hoselitz (ed.), The Progress of Underdeveloped Areas, University of Chicago Press, Chicago, 3-29.

Gersovitz, Mark (1983), Savings and Nutrition at Low Incomes, *Journal of Political Economy*, Vol. 91, 841-55.

Gersovitz, Mark (1988), Saving and Development, Handbook of Development Economics, Volume I, H. Chenery and T. N. Srinivasan (eds.), Elsevier Science Publishers, Amsterdam, 382-424.

Giovannini, Alberto (1985), Saving and the Real Interest Rate in LDCs, *Journal of Development Economics*, Vol. 18, 197-217.

Hahn, Frank (1984), On the Notion of Equilibrium in Economics, Frank Hahn (ed.), Equilibrium and Macroeconomics, Basil Blackwell, Oxford.

Hemmer, Hans-Rimbert (1988), Wirtschaftsprobleme der Entwicklungsländer, Vahlen-Verlag, München.

Hicks, Norman (1979), Growth vs. Basic Needs: Is There a Trade-Off?, *World Development*, Vol. 7, 985-994.

Islam, Nazrul (1995), Growth Empirics: A Panel Data Approach, *Quarterly Journal of Economics*, Vol. CX, 1127-1170.

Jones, Larry E. and Rodolfo E. *Manuelli* (1990), A Convex Model of Equilibrium Growth: Theory and Policy Implications, *Journal of Political Economy*, Vol. 98, 1008-1038.

Jones, Larry E. and Rodolfo E. *Manuelli* (1997), The Sources of Growth, *Journal of Economic Dynamics and Control*, Vol. 21, 75-114.

Kaldor, Nicholas (1961), Capital Accumulation and Economic Growth, F.A. Lutz and D.C. Hagur (eds.), The Theory of Capital, New York, St. Martin's Press, 177-222.

Kamien, Morton I. and Nancy L. *Schwartz* (1981), Dynamic Optimization, The Calculus of Variations and Optimal Control in Economics and Management, North-Holland, Amsterdam.

King, Robert G. and Sergio *Rebelo* (1993), Transitional Dynamics and Economic Growth in the Neoclassical Model, *American Economic Review*, Vol. 83, 908-931.

Kirman, Alan P. (1992), Whom or What Does the Representative Individual Represent?, *Journal of Economic Perspectives*, Vol. 6, 117-136.

Klein, L.R. and H. *Rubin* (1948-49), A Constant Utility Index of the Cost of Living, *Review of Economic Studies*, Vol. 15, 84-87.

Klenow, Peter and Andrés *Rodríguez-Clare* (1997), Economic Growth: A Review Essay, *Journal of Monetary Economics*, Vol. 40, 597-617.

Koch, Karl-Josef (1997), Mathematical Methods in the Theory of Economic Growth: Some Supplementary Remarks, Manuscript, University of Siegen.

Koch, Karl-Josef (1999), On the Analysis of Asymptotic Balanced Growth, Manuscript, University of Siegen.

Kocherlakota, Narayana R. and Kei-Mu *Yi* (1995), Can Convergence Regressions Distinguish between Exogenous and Endogenous Growth Models?, *Economic Letters*, Vol. 49, 211-215.

Koopmans, Tjalling C. (1965), On the Concept of Optimal Economic Growth, in: The Econometric Approach to Development Planning, North-Holland Publ. Co. and Rand-McNally, 1966 reissue of Pontificiae Academia Scientiarum Scripta Varia, Vol. 28, 225-300.

Kormendi, Roger C. and Philip G. *Meguire* (1985), Macroeconomic Determinants of Economic Growth: Cross-Country Evidence, *Journal of Monetary Economics*, Vol. 16, 141-163.

Kuznets, Simon (1973), Modern Economic Growth: Findings and Reflections, *American Economic Review*, Vol. 63, 247-258.

Ladrón-de-Guevara, Antonio, Salvador *Ortigueira*, and Manuel S. *Santos* (1997), Equilibrium Dynamics in Two-Sector Models of Endogenous Growth, *Journal of Economic Dynamics and Control*, Vol. 21, 115-143.

Lakatos, Imre (1978), The Methodology of Scientific Research Programmes, Philosophical Papers, J. Worrall and G. Currie (eds.), Vols. 1 and 2, Cambridge University Press, Cambridge MA.

Lazear, Edward (1977), Education: Consumption or Production?, *Journal of Political Economy*, Vol. 85, 569-597.

Leibenstein, Harvey A. (1957), Economic Backwardness and Economic Growth, Wiley, New York.

Levine, Ross and David *Renelt* (1992), A Sensitivity Analysis of Cross-Country Growth Regressions, *American Economic Review*, Vol. 82, 942-963.

Lorenz, Hans-Walter (1989), Nonlinear Dynamical Economics and Chaotic Motion, Springer-Verlag, Berlin.

Lucas, Robert E. Jr. (1988), On the Mechanics of Economic Development, *Journal of Monetary Economics*, Vol. 22, 3-42.

Lucas, Robert E. Jr. (1990), Why Doesn't Capital Flow from Rich to Poor Countries? *American Economic Association, Papers and Proceedings*, Vol. 80, 92-96.

Maddison, Angus (1979), Per Capita Output in the Long Run, *Kyklos*, Vol. 32, 412-429.

Mankiw, Gregory N. (1995), The Growth of Nations, *Brookings Papers on Economic Activity*, 1/1995, 275-326.

Mankiw, Gregory N., David *Romer*, and David N. *Weil* (1992), A Contribution to the Empirics of Economic Growth, *The Quarterly Journal of Economics*, May, 407-437.

Maußner, Alfred and Rainer *Klump* (1996), Wachstumstheorie, Springer-Verlag, Berlin.

Mikesell, Raymond F. and James E. *Zinser* (1973), The Nature of the Saving Function in Developing Countries: A Survey of the Theoretical and Empirical Literature, *Journal of Economic Literature*, Vol. 11, 1-26.

Nelson, Richard R. (1956), A Theory of the Low-Level Equilibrium Trap in Underdeveloped Economies, *American Econmomic Review*, Vol. 46, 894-908.

North, Douglas (1987), Institutions, Transactions Costs and Economic Growth, *Economic Enquiry*, Vol. 25, 419-428.

North, Douglas C. (1989), Institutions and Economic Growth: A Historical Introduction, *World Development*, Vol. 17, 1319-1322.

Nurkse, Ragnar (1962, first edition: 1953), Problems of Capital Formation in Underdeveloped Countries, Basil Blackwell, Oxford.

Obstfeld, Maurice (1990), Intertemporal Dependence, Impatience, and Dynamics, *Journal of Monetary Economics*, Vol. 26, 45-75.

Ogaki, Masao, Jonathan D. *Ostry*, and Carmen M. *Reinhart* (1996), Saving Behaviour in Low- and Middle-Income Developing Countries, A Comparison, *IMF Staff Papers*, Vol. 43, 38-71.

Ortigueira, Salvador and Manuel S. *Santos* (1997), On the Speed of Convergence in Endogenous Growth Models, *American Economic Review*, Vol. 87, 383-399.

Pack, Howard (1994), Endogenous Growth Theory: Intellectual Appeal and Empirical Shortcomings, *Journal of Economic Perspectives*, Vol. 8, 55-72.

Phelps, Edmund (1987), Equilibrium: An Expectational Concept, The New Palgrave: A Dictionary of Economics, J. Eatwell, M. Milgate, P. Newman (eds.), The Macmillan Press, New York, 177-179.

Pindyck, Robert S. and Daniel L. *Rubinfeld* (1991), Econometric Models & Economic Forecasts, McGraw-Hill, New York.

Popper, Karl R. (1967), Das Rationalitätsprinzip, reprinted in: Popper, Karl R. (1995), Lesebuch: Ausgewählte Texte zu Erkenntnistheorie, Philosophie der Naturwissenschaften, Metaphysik, Sozialphilosophie, David Miller (ed.), Mohr, Tübingen.

Popper, Karl R. (1973, first edition: 1934), Die Logik der Forschung, Mohr, Tübingen.

Pritchett, Lant (1996), Forget Convergence: Divergence Past, Present, and Future, *Finance and Development*, Vol. 33, 40-43.

Pritchett, Lant (1997), Divergence, Big Time, *Journal of Economic Perspectives*, Vol. 11, 3-17.

Pritchett, Lant (1998), Patterns of Economic Growth: Hills, Plateaus, Mountains, and Plains, Manuscript, World Bank, Washington DC.

Quah, Danny T. (1996), Twin Peaks: Growth and Convergence in Models of Distribution Dynamics, *The Economic Journal*, Vol. 106, 1045-1055.

Ram, Rati and Theodore W. *Schultz* (1979), Life Span, Health, Savings, and Productivity, *Economic Development and Cultural Change*, Vol. 27, 399-421.

Ramsey, Frank P. (1928), A Mathematical Theory of Saving, *The Economic Journal*, Vol. 38, 543-559. Reprinted in: Stiglitz, Joseph E. and Hirofumi Uzawa (eds.), Readings in the Modern Theory of Economic Growth, MIT Press, 1969.

Ravallion, Martin (1992), Poverty Comparisons — A Guide to Concepts and Methods, *LSMS Working Paper* No. 88, The World Bank, Washington DC.

Rebelo, Sergio (1991), Long-Run Policy Analysis and Long Run Growth, *Journal of Political Economy*, Vol. 99, 500-521.

Rebelo, Sergio (1992), Growth in Open Economies, *Carnegie Rochester Conference Series on Public Policy*, Vol. 36, 5-46.

Reichel, Richard (1993), Die Sparquote in Entwicklungs- und Schwellenländern, Determinanten und Möglichkeiten der wirtschaftspolitischen Beeinflussung, Paul Haupt, Bern.

Reynolds, Lloyd G. (1983), The Spread of Economic Growth to the Third World: 1850-1980, *Journal of Economic Literature*, Vol. 21, 941-980.

Rinne, Horst (1976), Ökonometrie, Kohlhammer, Stuttgart.

Romer, David (1996), Advanced Macroeconomics, McGraw-Hill, New York.

Romer, Paul M. (1986), Increasing Returns and Long-Run Growth, *Journal of Political Economy*, Vol. 94, 1002-1037.

Romer, Paul M. (1989), Capital Accumulation in the Theory of Long-Run Growth, R. J. Barro (ed.), Modern Business Cycle Theory, Basil Blackwell, Oxford, 51-127.

Romer, Paul M. (1990), Endogenous Technological Change, *Journal of Political Economy*, Vol. 98, 71-102.

Romer, Paul M. (1993), Idea Gaps and Object Gaps in Economic Development, *Journal of Monetary Economics*, Vol. 32, 543-573.

Rook, Marion, Dieter *Frey*, and Martin *Irle* (1993), Wissenschaftstheoretische Grundlagen sozialpsychologischer Wahrnehmung, Frey, D. and M. Irle (eds.), Theorien der Sozialpsychologie, Verlag Hans Huber, Bern.

Rosenzweig, Mark R. (1988), Labor Markets in Low-Income Countries, Handbook of Development Economics, Volume I, H. Chenery and T. N. Srinivasan (eds.), Elsevier Science Publishers, Amsterdam, 714-762.

Rostow, Walt W. (1956), The Take-Off into Self Sustained Growth, *The Economic Journal*, Vol. 66, 25-48.

Sala-i-Martin, Xavier X. (1990), On Growth and States, Ph.D. Dissertation, Harvard University.

Sala-i-Martin, Xavier X. (1996a), Regional Cohesion: Evidence and Theories of Regional Growth and Convergence, *European Economic Review*, Vol. 40, 1325-1352.

Sala-i-Martin, Xavier X. (1996b), The Classical Approach to Convergence Analysis, *The Economic Journal*, Vol. 106, 1019-1036.

Samuelson, Paul A. (1948-49), Some Implications of Linearity, *Review of Economic Studies*, Vol. 15, 88-90.

Sarel, Michael (1994), On the Dynamics of Economic Growth, *IMF Working Paper*, No. 138.

Sharif, Mohammed (1986), The Concept and Measurement of Subsistence: A Survey of the Literature, *World Development*, Vol. 14, 555-577.

Silberberg, Eugene (1990), The Structure of Economics: A Mathematical Analysis, McGraw Hill, New York.

Solow, Robert M. (1956), A Contribution to the Theory of Economic Growth, *Quarterly Journal of Economics*, Vol. 70, 65-94.

Steger, Thomas M. (2000a), Economic Growth with Subsistence Consumption, forthcoming in: *Journal of Development Economics*.

Steger, Thomas M. (2000b), Productive Consumption and Growth in Developing Countries, forthcoming in: *Review of Development Economics*.

Steger, Thomas M. (2000c), Transitional Dynamics with Endogenous Control Variables, forthcoming in: *Swiss Journal of Economics and Statistics*, Vol. 1/2000.

Stigler, George (1945), The Cost of Subsistence, *Journal of Farm Economics*, Vol. 27, 303-314.

Stiglitz, Joseph (1976), The Efficiency Wage Hypothesis, Surplus Labour, and the Distribution of Income in LDCs, *Oxford Economic Papers*, Vol. 28, 185-207.

Stone, Richard (1954), Linear Expenditure Systems and Demand Analysis: An Application to the Pattern of British Demand, *The Economic Journal*, Vol. 64, 511-527.

Strauss, John (1986), Does Better Nutrition Raise Farm Productivity?, *Journal of Political Economy*, Vol. 94, 297-320.

Summers, Robert and Alan *Heston* (1988), A New Set of International Comparisons of Real Product and Price Levels Estimate for 130 Countries 1950-1985, *Review of Income and Wealth*, Vol. 34, 1-25.

Summers, Robert and Alan *Heston* (1991), The Penn World Table (Mark 5): An Expanded Set of International Comparisons, 1950-1988, *Quarterly Journal of Economics*, Vol. 106 , 327-368.

Summers, Robert and Alan *Heston* (1999), The Penn World Table Mark 5.6, available e.g. at: http://arcadia.chass.utoronto.ca/pwt/.

Swan, Trevor W. (1956), Economic Growth and Capital Accumulation, *Economic Record*, Vol. 32, 334-361.

Temple, Jonathan (1998), Equipment Investment and the Solow Model, *Oxford Economic Papers*, Vol. 50, 39-62.

Temple, Jonathan (1999), The New Growth Evidence, *Journal of Economic Literature*, forthcoming.

Thirlwall, Anthony P. (1974), Inflation, Saving and Growth in Developing Economies, St. Martin's Press, New York.

Todaro, Michael P. (1994), Economic Development, Longman Publishing, New York.

Turnovsky, Stephen J. (1996), Methods of Macroeconomic Dynamics, MIT Press, Cambridge MA.

United Nations Development Program (1992), Human Development Report 1992, Oxford University Press, New York.

Wheeler, David (1980), Basic Needs Fulfilment and Economic Growth: A Simultaneous Model, *Journal of Development Economics*, Vol. 7, 435-451.

Wichmann, Thorsten (1996), Food Consumption and Growth in a Two Sector Economy, *Technical University Berlin Discussion Paper*, 1996/02.

Wichmann, Thorsten (1997), Agricultural Technical Progress and the Development of a Dual Economy, Physica-Verlag, Heidelberg.

Winslow, Charles-Edward A. (1951), The Cost of Sickness and the Price of Health, World Health Organization, Geneva.

Wolgenmuth, June C., Michael C. *Latham*, Andrew *Hall*, Andrew *Chesher*, and D. W. T. *Crompton* (1982), Worker Productivity and the Nutritional Status of Keynian Road Construction Labourer, *American Journal of Clinical Nutrition*, Vol. 36, 68-78.

World Bank (1990), World Development Report 1990: Poverty, Oxford University Press, New York.

World Bank (1994), World Development Report 1994, Oxford University Press, New York.

World Bank (1998), World Development Indicators, World Bank, Washington DC.

Yellen, Janet L. (1984), Efficiency Wage Models of Unemployment, *American Economic Association, Papers and Proceedings*, Vol. 74, 200-205.

Young, Alwyn (1995), The Tyranny of Numbers: Confronting the Statistical Realities of the East Asian Growth Experience, *The Quarterly Journal of Economics*, Vol. 110, 641-680.

Zee, Howell H. (1994), Endogenous Time Preference and Endogenous Growth, *IMF Working Paper*, January 1994 .

Zind, Richard G. (1991), Income Convergence and Divergence within and between LDC Groups, *World Development*, Vol. 19, 719-727.

List of figures

List of tables

Abbreviations

BGP	balanced-growth path
BGB$^{\infty}$	asymptotic balanced-growth path
DBGP$^{\infty}$	direction of asymptotic balanced-growth path
CES	constant elasticity of substitution
CIES	constant intertemporal elasticity of substitution
DCs	developing countries
eIES	effective intertemporal elasticity of substitution
GDP	gross domestic product
GNP	gross national product
IES	intertemporal elasticity of substitution
LDCs	less developed countries
NCC	net cost of consumption
OLS	ordinary least sqare
TSLS	two stage least-sqare

Lecture Notes in Economics and Mathematical Systems

For information about Vols. 1–295
please contact your bookseller or Springer-Verlag

Vol. 388: D. Bartmann, M. J. Beckmann, Inventory Control. XV, 252 pages. 1992.

Vol. 389: B. Dutta, D. Mookherjee, T. Parthasarathy, T. Raghavan, D. Ray, S. Tijs (Eds.), Game Theory and Economic Applications. Proceedings, 1990. IX, 454 pages. 1992.

Vol. 390: G. Sorger, Minimum Impatience Theorem for Recursive Economic Models. X, 162 pages. 1992.

Vol. 391: C. Keser, Experimental Duopoly Markets with Demand Inertia. X, 150 pages. 1992.

Vol. 392: K. Frauendorfer, Stochastic Two-Stage Programming. VIII, 228 pages. 1992.

Vol. 393: B. Lucke, Price Stabilization on World Agricultural Markets. XI, 274 pages. 1992.

Vol. 394: Y.-J. Lai, C.-L. Hwang, Fuzzy Mathematical Programming. XIII, 301 pages. 1992.

Vol. 395: G. Haag, U. Mueller, K. G. Troitzsch (Eds.), Economic Evolution and Demographic Change. XVI, 409 pages. 1992.

Vol. 396: R. V. V. Vidal (Ed.), Applied Simulated Annealing. VIII, 358 pages. 1992.

Vol. 397: J. Wessels, A. P. Wierzbicki (Eds.), User-Oriented Methodology and Techniques of Decision Analysis and Support. Proceedings, 1991. XII, 295 pages. 1993.

Vol. 398: J.-P. Urbain, Exogeneity in Error Correction Models. XI, 189 pages. 1993.

Vol. 399: F. Gori, L. Geronazzo, M. Galeotti (Eds.), Nonlinear Dynamics in Economics and Social Sciences. Proceedings, 1991. VIII, 367 pages. 1993.

Vol. 400: H. Tanizaki, Nonlinear Filters. XII, 203 pages. 1993.

Vol. 401: K. Mosler, M. Scarsini, Stochastic Orders and Applications. V, 379 pages. 1993.

Vol. 402: A. van den Elzen, Adjustment Processes for Exchange Economies and Noncooperative Games. VII, 146 pages. 1993.

Vol. 403: G. Brennscheidt, Predictive Behavior. VI, 227 pages. 1993.

Vol. 404: Y.-J. Lai, Ch.-L. Hwang, Fuzzy Multiple Objective Decision Making. XIV, 475 pages. 1994.

Vol. 405: S. Komlósi, T. Rapcsák, S. Schaible (Eds.), Generalized Convexity. Proceedings, 1992. VIII, 404 pages. 1994.

Vol. 406: N. M. Hung, N. V. Quyen, Dynamic Timing Decisions Under Uncertainty. X, 194 pages. 1994.

Vol. 407: M. Ooms, Empirical Vector Autoregressive Modeling. XIII, 380 pages. 1994.

Vol. 408: K. Haase, Lotsizing and Scheduling for Production Planning. VIII, 118 pages. 1994.

Vol. 409: A. Sprecher, Resource-Constrained Project Scheduling. XII, 142 pages. 1994.

Vol. 410: R. Winkelmann, Count Data Models. XI, 213 pages. 1994.

Vol. 411: S. Dauzère-Péres, J.-B. Lasserre, An Integrated Approach in Production Planning and Scheduling. XVI, 137 pages. 1994.

Vol. 412: B. Kuon, Two-Person Bargaining Experiments with Incomplete Information. IX, 293 pages. 1994.

Vol. 413: R. Fiorito (Ed.), Inventory, Business Cycles and Monetary Transmission. VI, 287 pages. 1994.

Vol. 414: Y. Crama, A. Oerlemans, F. Spieksma, Production Planning in Automated Manufacturing. X, 210 pages. 1994.

Vol. 415: P. C. Nicola, Imperfect General Equilibrium. XI, 167 pages. 1994.

Vol. 416: H. S. J. Cesar, Control and Game Models of the Greenhouse Effect. XI, 225 pages. 1994.

Vol. 417: B. Ran, D. E. Boyce, Dynamic Urban Transportation Network Models. XV, 391 pages. 1994.

Vol. 418: P. Bogetoft, Non-Cooperative Planning Theory. XI, 309 pages. 1994.

Vol. 419: T. Maruyama, W. Takahashi (Eds.), Nonlinear and Convex Analysis in Economic Theory. VIII, 306 pages. 1995.

Vol. 420: M. Peeters, Time-To-Build. Interrelated Investment and Labour Demand Modelling. With Applications to Six OECD Countries. IX, 204 pages. 1995.

Vol. 421: C. Dang, Triangulations and Simplicial Methods. IX, 196 pages. 1995.

Vol. 422: D. S. Bridges, G. B. Mehta, Representations of Preference Orderings. X, 165 pages. 1995.

Vol. 423: K. Marti, P. Kall (Eds.), Stochastic Programming. Numerical Techniques and Engineering Applications. VIII, 351 pages. 1995.

Vol. 424: G. A. Heuer, U. Leopold-Wildburger, Silverman's Game. X, 283 pages. 1995.

Vol. 425: J. Kohlas, P.-A. Monney, A Mathematical Theory of Hints. XIII, 419 pages, 1995.

Vol. 426: B. Finkenstädt, Nonlinear Dynamics in Economics. IX, 156 pages. 1995.

Vol. 427: F. W. van Tongeren, Microsimulation Modelling of the Corporate Firm. XVII, 275 pages. 1995.

Vol. 428: A. A. Powell, Ch. W. Murphy, Inside a Modern Macroeconometric Model. XVIII, 424 pages. 1995.

Vol. 429: R. Durier, C. Michelot, Recent Developments in Optimization. VIII, 356 pages. 1995.

Vol. 430: J. R. Daduna, I. Branco, J. M. Pinto Paixão (Eds.), Computer-Aided Transit Scheduling. XIV, 374 pages. 1995.

Vol. 431: A. Aulin, Causal and Stochastic Elements in Business Cycles. XI, 116 pages. 1996.

Vol. 432: M. Tamiz (Ed.), Multi-Objective Programming and Goal Programming. VI, 359 pages. 1996.

Vol. 433: J. Menon, Exchange Rates and Prices. XIV, 313 pages. 1996.

Vol. 434: M. W. J. Blok, Dynamic Models of the Firm. VII, 193 pages. 1996.

Vol. 435: L. Chen, Interest Rate Dynamics, Derivatives Pricing, and Risk Management. XII, 149 pages. 1996.

Vol. 436: M. Klemisch-Ahlert, Bargaining in Economic and Ethical Environments. IX, 155 pages. 1996.

Vol. 437: C. Jordan, Batching and Scheduling. IX, 178 pages. 1996.

Vol. 438: A. Villar, General Equilibrium with Increasing Returns. XIII, 164 pages. 1996.

Vol. 439: M. Zenner, Learning to Become Rational. VII, 201 pages. 1996.

Vol. 440: W. Ryll, Litigation and Settl ent in a Ga with Incomplete Information. VIII, 174 pa s. 1996.

Vol. 441: H. Dawid, Adaptive L rning y Algorithms. IX, 166 pages.1996.

Vol. 442: L. Corchón, Theories of Imperfectly Competitive Markets. XIII, 163 pages. 1996.

Vol. 443: G. Lang, On Overlapping Generations Models with Productive Capital. X, 98 pages. 1996.

Vol. 444: S. Jørgensen, G. Zaccour (Eds.), Dynamic Competitive Analysis in Marketing. X, 285 pages. 1996.

Vol. 445: A. H. Christer, S. Osaki, L. C. Thomas (Eds.), Stochastic Modelling in Innovative Manufactoring. X, 361 pages. 1997.

Vol. 446: G. Dhaene, Encompassing. X, 160 pages. 1997.

Vol. 447: A. Artale, Rings in Auctions. X, 172 pages. 1997.

Vol. 448: G. Fandel, T. Gal (Eds.), Multiple Criteria Decision Making. XII, 678 pages. 1997.

Vol. 449: F. Fang, M. Sanglier (Eds.), Complexity and Self-Organization in Social and Economic Systems. IX, 317 pages, 1997.

Vol. 450: P. M. Pardalos, D. W. Hearn, W. W. Hager, (Eds.), Network Optimization. VIII, 485 pages, 1997.

Vol. 451: M. Salge, Rational Bubbles. Theoretical Basis, Economic Relevance, and Empirical Evidence with a Special Emphasis on the German Stock Market.IX, 265 pages. 1997.

Vol. 452: P. Gritzmann, R. Horst, E. Sachs, R. Tichatschke (Eds.), Recent Advances in Optimization. VIII, 379 pages. 1997.

Vol. 453: A. S. Tangian, J. Gruber (Eds.), Constructing Scalar-Valued Objective Functions. VIII, 298 pages. 1997.

Vol. 454: H.-M. Krolzig, Markov-Switching Vector Auto-regressions. XIV, 358 pages. 1997.

Vol. 455: R. Caballero, F. Ruiz, R. E. Steuer (Eds.), Advances in Multiple Objective and Goal Programming. VIII, 391 pages. 1997.

Vol. 456: R. Conte, R. Hegselmann, P. Terna (Eds.), Simulating Social Phenomena. VIII, 536 pages. 1997.

Vol. 457: C. Hsu, Volume and the Nonlinear Dynamics of Stock Returns. VIII, 133 pages. 1998.

Vol. 458: K. Marti, P. Kall (Eds.), Stochastic Programming Methods and Technical Applications. X, 437 pages. 1998.

Vol. 459: H. K. Ryu, D. J. Slottje, Measuring Trends in U.S. Income Inequality. XI, 195 pages. 1998.

Vol. 460: B. Fleischmann, J. A. E. E. van Nunen, M. G. Speranza, P. Stähly, Advances in Distribution Logistic. XI, 535 pages. 1998.

Vol. 461: U. Schmidt, Axiomatic Utility Theory under Risk. XV, 201 pages. 1998.

Vol. 462: L. von Auer, Dynamic Preferences, Choice Mechanisms, and Welfare. XII, 226 pages. 1998.

Vol. 463: G. Abraham-Frois (Ed.), Non-Linear Dynamics and Endogenous Cycles. VI, 204 pages. 1998.

Vol. 464: A. Aulin, The Impact of Science on Economic Growth and its Cycles. IX, 204 pages. 1998.

Vol. 465: ". ' Stewart, 1 an den Honert (Eds.), Trends ulti te... Decision N ng. X, 448 pages. 1998.

'. 466: A. Sadrieh, The Alternating Double Auction et. VII, 350 pages. 1998.

... 467: H. Hennig-Schmidt, Bargaining in a Video Experiment. Determinants of Boundedly Rational Behavior. XII, 221 pages. 1999.

Vol. 468: A. Ziegler, A Game Theory Analysis of Options. XIV, 145 pages. 1999.

Vol. 469: M. P. Vogel, Environmental Kuznets Curves. XIII, 197 pages. 1999.

Vol. 470: M. Ammann, Pricing Derivative Credit Risk. XII, 228 pages. 1999.

Vol. 471: N. H. M. Wilson (Ed.), Computer-Aided Transit Scheduling. XI, 444 pages. 1999.

Vol. 472: J.-R. Tyran, Money Illusion and Strategic Complementarity as Causes of Monetary Non-Neutrality. X, 228 pages. 1999.

Vol. 473: S. Helber, Performance Analysis of Flow Lines with Non-Linear Flow of Material. IX, 280 pages. 1999.

Vol. 474: U. Schwalbe, The Core of Economies with Asymmetric Information. IX, 141 pages. 1999.

Vol. 475: L. Kaas, Dynamic Macroeconomics with Imperfect Competition. XI, 155 pages. 1999.

Vol. 476: R. Demel, Fiscal Policy, Public Debt and the Term Structure of Interest Rates. X, 279 pages. 1999.

Vol. 477: M. Théra, R. Tichatschke (Eds.), Ill-posed Variational Problems and Regularization Techniques. VIII, 274 pages. 1999.

Vol. 478: S. Hartmann, Project Scheduling under Limited Resources. XII, 221 pages. 1999.

Vol. 479: L. v. Thadden, Money, Inflation, and Capital Formation. IX, 192 pages. 1999.

Vol. 480: M. Grazia Speranza, P. Stähly (Eds.), New Trends in Distribution Logistics. X, 336 pages. 1999.

Vol. 481: V. H. Nguyen, J. J. Strodiot, P. Tossings (Eds.). Optimation. IX, 498 pages. 2000.

Vol. 482: W. B. Zhang, A Theory of International Trade. XI, 192 pages. 2000.

Vol. 483: M. Königstein, Equity, Efficiency and Evolutionary Stability in Bargaining Games with Joint Production. XII, 197 pages. 2000.

Vol. 484: D. D. Gatti, M. Gallegati, A. Kirman, Interaction and Market Structure. VI, 298 pages. 2000.

Vol. 485: A. Garnaev, Search Games and Other Applications of Game Theory. VIII, 145 pages. 2000.

Vol. 486: M. Neugart, Nonlinear Labor Market Dynamics. X, 175 pages. 2000.

Vol. 487: Y. Y. Haimes, R. E. Steuer (Eds.), Research and Practice in Multiple Criteria Decision Making. XVII, 553 pages. 2000.

Vol. 488: B. Schmolck, Ommitted Variable Tests and Dynamic Specification. X, 144 pages. 2000.

Vol. 489: T. Steger, Transitional Dynamics and Economic Growth in Developing Countries. VIII, 151 pages. 2000.